Little Visits
with Jesus

# Little Visits with Jesus

### Devotions for Families with Young Children

## By Mary Manz Simon

### Illustrated by Arthur W. Kirchhoff

Publishing House
St. Louis

# Printing History

| Year | Paperback | Hardback | Combined | Total |
|------|-----------|----------|----------|-------|
| 1987 | 20,000 | 5,000 | 25,000 | 25,000 |
| 1988 | 10,000 | 10,000 | 20,000 | 45,000 |
| 1989 | 15,000 | - | 15,000 | 60,000 |

For our children—
Christy, Angela, and Matthew
Psalm 127:3

Scripture quotations are from the Good News Bible, the Bible in TODAY'S ENGLISH VER-
SION. Copyright © American Bible Society 1966, 1971, 1976. Used by permission.

Copyright © 1987 Concordia Publishing House
3558 S. Jefferson Avenue, St. Louis, MO 63118-3968
Manufactured in the United States of America

Library of Congress Cataloging in Publication Data

Simon, Mary Manz, 1948–
    Little visits with Jesus.

    Summary: Two hundred forty daily devotions, grouped by months of the year, to nurture
Christian faith and life.
    1. Children—Prayer-books and devotions—English. 2. Family—Prayer-books and devo-
tions—English. [1. Prayer books and devotions. 2. Christian life]
I. Title.
BV870.S54 1987   242′.2   87-9154
ISBN 0-570-03075-7

4 5 6 7 8 9 10 11 12 13  IB  99 98 97 96 95 94 93 92 91 90

# Contents

**Preface**                                                    9
**Suggestions for Use**                                        11
**Devotions:**
**January**                                                    13

Happy New Year                    Nightmares
It's No Joke                      Where's the Piece?
Daddies and Fathers               A Corner of Heaven
Church Time Again?                Will the Fairy Come?
Day Number Eleven                 All About J
Happy "Old Christmas"             Are You a Show-Off?
Special Time                      Our Powerful God
Friends                           Happy Birthday to Me
A Cross Search                    What's Your Favorite Snack?
Thanks, God!                      Remember Christmas?

**February**                                                   33

A Band-Aid Day                    It's Coming!
Where?                            Introducing Me!
An Easy Way?                      Love Day
Loving All Your Life              St. Valentine's Day
A Stormy Night                    St. Valentine's Day, Again!
Surprises                         Nothing Special?
Feed the Birds                    Wear Jesus
Counting Pennies                  A Fire
Mommy's Hard Day                  Have a Problem?
A Winter Vacation                 A February Surprise

**March**                                                      53

A Late Valentine                  Upside Down, Inside Out
Bored?                            Where Is Spring?
Signs Without Words               Play-Dough Pretending
What If?                          I Need Christmas
Pets                              Happy Spring!
Sharing a Dustpan                 Looking Ahead
It's Pretzel Day!                 Scary Things
It's Dropping!                    Bumps and Itches
Don't Climb the Flowers!          No Wrinkles in Heaven
Zebras and Children               A Present for Easter

84069

**April**     **73**

Easter Egg Cartons
Some Easter Fun
Playing Easter
Another Easter?
Olden Day Easters
No Easter Bunny?
Animal Riddles
Afraid of the Dark
Hooray! Hooray!
Planting Time

**May**

Those Wonderful Eyes
I Hate Rain!
Egg Talk
Voices in the Night
"A" Is for Animal
Car Wash Time
A Spring Walk
It's Cleaning Day
Growing Bigger, Growing
   Smaller
Shadow Play

**June**     **113**

Balloons in Heaven?
Thanks, God, for Goldfish
All Gone
Magic Carpets
Worried?
"I'm So Tired!"
Snack on a Stick
Joe and His Coat
A Ducky Day!
Alone in a Crowd?

**July**

Moving Around
My Home
A Good Game?

You Can't See It, but . . .
Just the Two of Us
Why?
At the Airport
Who Is It?
Shopping Time
Earth Week at Danielle's House
Let's Play!
Somebody Knows Your Secret
Why Do I Have to Grow Up?
    **93**

Be Alive!
Thumbs Up!
Rush Here, Rush There
See What I Can Do!
"It's Not Warm Enough!"
Keep God's World Beautiful
What Comes First?
The Original Helmet
A Present That's Not Wrapped
Seein' Green

Underground Food
Time for Bed
'Round and 'Round
Alike and Different
Map Fun
Grown-up Jobs
Why Does the Sun Shine?
A Good Kind of Tired
Half and Half
A Special Friend
    **133**

A Muddy-Muddy-Muddy
"When Will I Read?"
A Sit-Down Summer

It's Always Hot     A Special Reminder
Keeping Cool     Playing Statues
Summer Sillies     Twinkling Christmas Lights
A Good Helper     Flying High
No Lights!     $$$$$$
"Pack Up—Let's Go!"     Listen to Love
A Thank-You Day     Water, Water Everywhere

**August**     **153**
Make a "Good Book"     Thinking of You
A Smelly Hike     Box City
Fix-it Time     A Liquid Lunch
Out for Breakfast     A Bible Bookworm
Will You Die?     The Shivers!
Amen, Amen     Good Smells
Home, Sweet Home     Mirror, Mirror
Smile Time     A Busy Dozen
Writing a Book     Let's Pretend
An Ice Day     Who Ever Listens to Me?

**September**     **173**
Miss Jellyface     A Singin' Saturday
What's in a Lunchbox?     I Forgive You
Sunday Best     A Leaf Hunt
A Letter for You     Hello and Good-bye
It's Autumn!     Jesus Is Near
Pick a Little Bit o' Christmas     The Wiggly, Squiggly Ones
A Sad September?     The Smell of September
Long Ago     A Look Through Julie's Eyes
Happy Rainbow Day!     A Good Question
Cooking Time     A Church Box

**October**     **193**
Changes, Changes     Not Too Little
Love, Love, Love     Something New
Move Over, Baby     Dress-Up
Who Knows It All?     A Job for Jesus
Don't Forget     Just Plain Me
Witness     Money to Give Away
About Dying     Laugh a Lot
Where Am I?     Lost and Found

Circles
It's Not Fair

No Witches! No Ghosts!
Knock, Knock

**November**                                        **213**

Shout It Out
Cleaning Up
Extra Thanks
Look Ahead!
Helping Each Other
Alone Time
Who Started It?
God's House
Calling You!
Rain, Rain, Go Away

Always God's Child
Call for Help
A Lousy Thanksgiving?
Plenty for All
Thanksgiving Every Day
Word Games
What a Rainbow World!
No Friends
A Brown Day
When?

**December**                                        **233**

All Kinds of Shoes
A Birthday Is to Share
Happy in Heaven
Good Night
Real or Pretend?
A True Story
Happy Times
A Frosty Picture
Happy Birthday, Dear Jesus
How Do You Open Up
    Christmas?

An Empty Christmas?
The Smell of Christmas
Sharing Can Be Tough
When Shoes Don't Fit
A Don't Day or a Do Day?
Window Shopping
Puddles
Nothing to Do
Growing Up and Up
Good-bye

**Scripture Index**                                 **253**
**Devotions for Special Days**                      **256**

# Preface

Our family's children really matter to me. I do everything possible to help them grow and develop. I'm aware of the importance of "bonding" with young children and that such time together has a positive influence on later relationships.

Young children also need a different, yet equally important bonding time—one with Jesus Christ. In our home we call it "Jesus time." During this time of the day we learn together about the Savior who lived, died, and rose for all, even for our three-year-old.

Family devotions are important. The practice says to children that faith is not just for Sunday mornings in church; it is part of daily living.

Because many families have few opportunities during the day when everyone can be together, family devotions also are a joy. "Jesus time" provides a daily opportunity for all of us to grow closer to each other as we grow spiritually closer to our Lord.

In whatever setting you use this book—around the kitchen table, on the edge of a bed, or in an early childhood classroom—I pray it will help you grow in your understanding of and relationship to a child whom you love and a God who loves you.

I also pray that your young child—God's gift to you—may enjoy a growing relationship both with you as a caring person and with the Savior of all, Jesus Christ.

*Mary Manz Simon*

# Suggestions for Use

1. While older children can benefit from these devotions, they are intended for use with young children. Use this book once your child is old enough to express feelings and thoughts in even a few words. We began developing these devotions when our son was less than a year old. At the time he probably didn't benefit from the content, but he did learn that we talk to Jesus every day. That's important for a person of any age.

2. Try to set aside one specific time each day for "Jesus Time"—bedtime, before breakfast, after mid-morning snacks, etc. These very brief devotions will fit into almost any schedule.

3. Twenty devotions are provided for each month—approximately five per week. This allows you the freedom to extend a devotion into a second day, to create your own based on an important family event, or to consider Sunday worship at church as that day's "Jesus Time." Also, since children mature rapidly at this age, repeating a devotion a month later will bring different responses and invite greater insights.

4. When possible, personalize the devotions as you use them. For example, substitute the name of your child for the name of the child in the devotion.

5. Whenever a devotion calls for responses, use whatever response your child offers to start a conversation, to extend your child's learning, or to clarify a meaning or feeling.

6. Scripture readings are listed at the top of the page, along with a pertinent excerpt. Whenever possible, read the selection from the Bible that belongs to your child. Or, as this book does, you might use Today's English Version (the *Good News Bible*) because of its simple language.

7. If you're using this devotion book in a classroom, you may want to enlarge some of the illustrations by tracing them onto a blank overhead transparency. Or select a large picture or poster expressing the same idea as the devotion's illustration.

8. The devotions assume active adult participation along with the children. When there are questions, talk about your responses as well as the children's. When an activity is suggested, participate with your child. In doing so, you too will grow in faith.

*His love is eternal.*
Psalm 118:29

# Happy New Year

Do you have a new calendar at your house? Today we start a new year. Sometimes, starting new things can be scary. Were you ever scared when you started something new? Were you ever excited when you started something new?

Today we start a new year. But we will eat the same kinds of food we ate last year. What would you like to eat this year?

You will probably have the same favorite toys. What will you like to play with this year?

You are still loved by Jesus. He will love you this year just as much as last year. Last year, this new year, and even next year, Jesus will love you.

# Dear Jesus,

It's a new year, and _____.

Some people get excited about New Year's Day, Jesus. I'm just glad You'll always be my Friend. Amen.

*I will never forget you.*
Isaiah 49:15

# It's No Joke

Holly and her friends were telling jokes. She asked, "What's green with red spots?"

"A polka-dot alligator," guessed one friend.

"A Christmas tree with red ornaments," guessed another.

What do you think is green with red spots?

"Well, Holly, what is green with red spots?" her friends asked impatiently.

"I can't remember!" said Holly. Everyone smiled.

We forget lots of things, but one thing we should always remember: Jesus is our Savior. That's no joke; that's for real—but it can still make us smile. (Holly just remembered the answer to the joke: What's green with red spots? A pickle with chicken pox.)

# Dear Jesus,

Thanks for giving me so many things to smile about. Amen.

*Obey your parents . . .*
Colossians 3:20

# Daddies and Fathers

"When I'm a daddy, can I yell?" Joshua James asked his father.

"Oh, Josh, is that all I do as a father?" his dad asked.

"Well, you sure yell loud when you're mad," Joshua James answered.

"Why do you think I yell?" his dad asked.

"'Cause sometimes I don't do what you tell me. If you yell that means I really need to obey," Joshua James said.

"That's right. But it's my turn to ask a question. Do you like it when I yell?"

"No!" said Joshua James.

"Then let's try something," said his dad. "I'll try not to yell when I'm angry. You can try to obey. Then we'll both feel better."

# Dear Jesus,

Help me obey my parents. I usually know what's right. Help me do what's right. Amen.

*Let us go to the Lord's house.*
Psalm 122:1

# Church Time Again?

Who works at your church? Listen to this story and see if you're surprised who works at Lioba's church.

"Hurry up, Lioba," her mother said. "We don't want to be late for church."

"Why do we have to go again?" Lioba asked. "We went at least a million times at Christmas. I'm tired of church."

"I need to go," her mother answered. "That's my time without the phone ringing or things to do. I can pray and work with God."

"That's silly," said Lioba. "How do you work with God when all you do is sit and be quiet?"

"I think about what is happening," said her mother. "I work inside my head. I think about what the words mean that I say and hear."

"Oh," said Lioba. "I never thought about my head working at church. I'll try that today."

What do you think about when you go to church?

# Dear Jesus,

I know that going to church can mean different things to different people. Some people like to hear the pretty music. Some like the nice windows. I like _____in church. Amen.

*Some men who studied the stars came from the East to Jerusalem.*
Matthew 2:1–2

## Day Number Eleven

Joel was going to love today. Today was the eleventh day after Christmas. Epiphany, or "Old Christmas Day" as Nana called it, was tomorrow.

The Magi had visited the Baby Jesus at the first Epiphany. To remember that time and the rich gifts brought to Jesus, Joel's family decorated the manger set at their house to look like a king was expected.

Nana gave Joel and Tammy a roll of foil paper. They got out the little bag they had stuffed with bits of fabric, papers, and tidbits saved during the year.

Tammy started to work on a shining thing with points. She folded the foil carefully. She was going to tape this foil item to a stick behind the crèche. It would look like it was in the sky. What do you think she was making now?

Joel worked with different bits of fabric. What do you think he was making?

## Dear Jesus,

Thank You that Christmas keeps going on and on . . . just like Your love for me. Amen.

*And so they left.*
Matthew 2:9–11

# Happy "Old Christmas"

Quickly Tammy hopped out and got dressed. The twelfth day after Christmas ("Old Christmas," as Nana called it) was busy at Tammy's house.

Tammy and her brother, Joel, worked most of the day with Nana to take down the Christmas decorations.

Finally everything was put away except the tree and manger. After supper everyone helped with that. Tammy loved to sing the carols one last time. Only the manger was left. Everyone gathered around to open the last present of the season. What fun to have another Christmas present!

Then Tammy and Joel bundled up to watch the cutting of the Christmas tree. The logs and bigger twigs were piled up carefully in a special place next to the wood pile. They would burn this Christmas tree in the fireplace next year on Christmas Day.

Now Christmas was really over. Tammy felt contented and satisfied when she went to bed that night. She wondered what other children in different parts of the world did on Old Christmas Day.

How do you celebrate the twelfth day after Christmas?

# Dear Jesus,

Prayer suggestion: Talk to Jesus about your day.

*I will remember Your great
deeds.* Psalm 77:11–12

## *Special Time*

Bedtime was Chad's favorite time of day. He had listened to a story, brushed his teeth, and said prayers with his mom.

Chad heard his mother go down the stairs. The hall light clicked on, just as it did every night. Now was his special time. This was Chad's "Jesus Time."

Chad laid in bed and remembered as many things as possible that had happened during the day. Then he talked quietly to Jesus. It was fun having a friend no one could see but who would still listen. Chad loved talking to Jesus all by himself.

## *Dear Jesus,*

Prayer suggestion: When is your special time alone with Jesus? Talk to Him now.

*Come with Me!*
John 1:43–46

# Friends

Shelly and Dana were best friends. They liked to do lots of things together. (What do you think Shelly and Dana played?)

They always had a great time. But one thing made Shelly very sad. Dana didn't go to church. On Sunday mornings Shelly could see Dana peeking through the window as Shelly's family left for church.

One day Shelly talked to her pastor about Dana. Shelly asked, "Pastor Hank, I want my friend to come to church. What should I do?"

What do you think Pastor Hank suggested?

# Dear Jesus,

Help me think of lots of different ways I can invite people to my church. I know I can mail invitations. We can even offer to bring people to church when we go. Help me to remember that going to church is even more fun when I go with a friend. Amen.

*He went out, carrying His
cross.* John 19:17–18

# A Cross Search

"That must be a Bible," said Alex, pointing to a book on the table.

"How do you know?" his grandmother asked.

"It has a cross on it," Alex answered. "That's what the Bible is all about: Jesus died on a cross."

"And look what I always wear," his grandmother said. "Your Grandpa gave me this necklace with a cross many years ago. I've never taken it off."

"Never?" Alex asked.

"Never," she answered. "Come now, let's see how many more crosses we can find."

Alex and his grandmother walked around the house. They found one cross with two circles on it in his parents' room.

"That was on your parents' wedding cake," his grandmother said.

Alex even found a cross outside the front door.

"That shows everybody that we love Jesus," said Alex.

Alex and his grandmother found four crosses at their house. How many crosses can you find at your house? Ask someone to help you look.

# Dear Jesus,

Help me always to remember what the cross means. Amen.

*Our Lord, Your greatness*
*is seen in all the world!*
Psalm 8:1, 3–4

# *Thanks, God!*

Here are some questions:

Why are train tunnels round?
Do birds cry?
How do stars shine?

Can you answer any of those questions? I can't without some help from good books.

I didn't even make up those questions. A little boy asked them.

What a good mind God gave that little boy! And what a wonderful mind God has given you!

You can ask questions. You can answer questions. You can look at pictures, read books, and go places that will help you learn many things about our world.

Today when you talk to Jesus, thank Him for a good mind. God has blessed *you* with the wonderful ability to think.

# *Dear Jesus,*

Thank You for letting me think. I like to think about some of my favorite things, like _____
_____ . Amen.

*Why are you so frightened?*
Matthew 8:23–27

# Nightmares

Harold sat up in bed. He was shaking. He was scared. "Don't make it come true; don't make it come true," Harold kept crying.

Harold had dreamed a bad nightmare. He was worried that what he dreamed about would really happen.

Have you ever had a bad dream? Talk about it to the person who is reading to you.

Jesus wants to hear about things that bother you, too. You can always talk to Him, even if no other people are around. He will hear you. Jesus will always listen.

# Dear Jesus,

Thank You for knowing how scared I sometimes get. Please help me remember I can always talk to You. Amen.

*Some friends are more loyal than brothers.* Proverbs 18:24

## Where's the Piece?

Outside the girls' room the weather was blustery. The wind blew cold air all around the house.

Inside the house Paula and Lana were warm and cozy. It was a perfect time to work a puzzle. Lana did the bottom half of the puzzle. Paula worked at the top. Carefully they fit together the two halves. But one piece was missing! They looked and looked. There was the piece: under the box lid. At last the puzzle was done.

How neat that felt! And what fun the girls had!

How do you spend wintry days?

## Dear Jesus,

Thank You for some of the things I forget to mention all the time: friends to play with; toys to use; and in winter, a place to keep warm. Amen.

*God will wipe away every
tear from their eyes.*
Revelation 7:16–17

# *A Corner of Heaven*

Angela started her prayers with this one night: "Dear God, please take care of Mr. Gain in heaven."

Mr. Gain was a friend of Angela. He had just died. Angela knew Mr. Gain was with Jesus in heaven, but she still wanted to talk to God about it.

Angela did something else. She drew a picture of Mr. Gain's corner of heaven. In heaven we will have everything we need, so Angela colored a picture of where she thought Mr. Gain was living with Jesus. In her picture Mr. Gain had a nice green riding mower and some new tools.

# *Dear Jesus,*

Prayer suggestion: Who has died whom you know? Draw their corner of heaven; then talk to Jesus about how you feel.

*How good it is to give*
*thanks to You, O Lord.*
Psalm 92:1

# Will the Fairy Come?

Bonnie wiggled and wiggled. She used her tongue to push, too. Finally her loose tooth came out.

Bonnie carefully wrapped up the tooth. She put it on her bed under the pillow. Bonnie hoped the tooth fairy would come that night and leave her some money.

Somebody watched all this. The peeker was Bobby. Bobby was Bonnie's little brother. He was three years old. Can you guess what Bobby did?

First Bobby tried to wiggle all his teeth. Nothing happened.

Then Bobby thought and thought and thought. Bobby went outside. He found a pine cone. He put the pine cone under his pillow.

Then Bobby went and told his mother, "Mommy, I'm all ready for the pine cone fairy to come tonight. The fairy will find a pine cone under my pillow and leave me some money!"

Do you think the pine cone fairy visited Bobby?

Sometimes we want something very much. First Bobby wanted to be like his older sister with a loose tooth. Then Bobby wanted to have a visit from a fairy.

What is something you wish for?

# Dear Jesus,

I know I can't have everything I want. Please help me to remember to say "thank you" when I get something. Please help me accept times when I can't have what I want. Amen.

*Praise His name with
dancing.* Psalm 149:1–3

# All About J

What is this letter? [Point to the letter J.]

J begins many words. See if you can answer these riddles. Each answer will start with a J.

You spread this on bread: _____

The name of this month: _____

A person you learn about at Sunday school: _____

Now do something that starts with J. _____

Did you jump? We can jump with joy because Jesus loves us. J starts lots of words, like jelly, jam, January, and jump.

J is for Jesus, too. And Jesus is the most important J word of all!

Jesus died on the cross for us. That's worth jumping for joy at least one more time. Ready, get set, jump!

# Dear Jesus,

I just jumped for joy. Just, jumped, and joy are J words. You are a J word too. Thank You for loving me. Amen.

*I will show you my*
*faith by my actions.*
James 2:18

# Are You a Show-Off?

"Show-off, show-off, you're just a show-off." Have you ever said those words? What is a show-off, anyway?

Sometimes being a show-off isn't good. It's not good to brag. But you can show off in some nice ways.

You can show a friend something new.

You can show someone you care by doing something nice.

You can ask a person to come see your church or Sunday school.

You can show someone you love them. Do that right now with the person who's reading this book.

What's another way you could show someone you love them?

# Dear Jesus,

Thank You for showing me how much You love me. You show me every day that You love me: When I do something wrong You forgive me. You showed me You love me when You died on the cross. You show me You love me when You put people around me who love me. Thank You, Jesus. Amen.

*Listen, all of you, to
the voice of God.* Job 37:1–5

# Our Powerful God

It was a stormy day. Even though it wasn't nighttime, the sky was dark, covered with big clouds. When a flash of lightning brightened the sky, Jacky said, "I think I know how God makes lightning. He uses a big flashlight."

A little later the thunder stopped. The lightning didn't flash anymore, and Jacky said, "It stopped raining. God turned off the faucets."

Jacky didn't really understand what caused the rain to fall and what made the lightning happen. (Ask an adult to help you find the answers.) But he was right about one thing: God is in charge. God is powerful. He made nature.

Now let's try something. Clap your hands. That's what happens when it thunders. Cold air bumps into warm air and makes a noise. That's just like what happens when one hand touches your other hand in a "clap." That's how God makes thunder.

Everything that happens in our weather isn't as easy to understand, but one thing is sure: God is in charge.

# Dear God,

Thank You for protecting me. Amen.

*See how much the Father
has loved us!* 1 John 3:1a

# Happy Birthday to Me

"Will I still be a kid after my birthday today?" Matthew asked his aunt.

"Yes," she smiled. "You still have years of being a kid, as you say."

"Will I still have blond hair after my birthday?" Matthew asked.

"Why, Matthew, of course," she replied. "You know, you've been blond since about your first birthday."

"Will I still . . . " Matthew started to ask, but his aunt interrupted.

"Oh, Matthew; don't ask more questions. I'll still love you, too, after your birthday. Now go ahead and play."

Someone else will still love Matthew, too. Can you think who that might be?

# Dear Jesus,

Thank You for always loving me. Amen.

*You give them food when*
*they need it.* Psalm 145:15–16

# What's Your Favorite Snack?

This is a true story of something that really happened. Listen and see if anything like this ever happened at your house:

"I'm hungry, Mommy," said Bobby.

"Have a piece of cheese," said Mommy.

"No, I'm hungry for something else," said Bobby.

"There's some blueberry yogurt in the refrigerator. Help yourself," said Mommy.

"No," said Bobby.

"How about a carrot?" Mommy offered. "I'll even peel it for you."

"No, no, no. That's all food that's good for you. I don't want it," said Bobby.

Did anything like this ever happen to you?

God gives us all kinds of food. He wants us to keep our bodies healthy. How do you thank God for your food? Show God, now.

# Dear Jesus,

Prayer suggestion: Use Psalm 145:15–16 as your table prayer.

*God sent His own Son.*
Galatians 4:4–5

## Remember Christmas?

Phyllis couldn't believe what she saw. As she and her mom were driving past church, Phyllis saw the Christmas stable was still out in front. It was empty. Mary, Joseph, Baby Jesus, and all the other figures were gone.

"Mommy, look," Phyllis said as she pointed out the window. "Why didn't they put away the stable at church?"

"I heard some people talking about that last week," her mother smiled. "All the manger figures that sat on top of the ground were put away after Epiphany. But the stable posts that are sunk underneath are frozen into the ground. The stable might be out there until spring."

"That's alright," said Phyllis. "It helps me remember Christmas."

What do you remember about Christmas?

## Dear Jesus,

I remember when it was Your birthday. Thank You for Christmas. Amen.

*I wait eagerly for the
Lord's help.* Psalm 130:1–2, 5

# A Band-Aid Day

Vincent had a tough morning. He woke up late. Then he put on one brown sock and one blue sock and had to do it over. The oatmeal was cold by the time he got to the breakfast table. The weather was cold, and Vincent had to wear the purple plaid scarf he didn't like. Then he tripped on some ice at the front sidewalk. Vincent walked carefully back to the front door to get a Band-Aid.

What else could happen to Vincent?

Next, he pinched his finger in the zipper on his backpack. He was trying to get a Kleenex for his nose; he had a cold.

Poor Vincent. Have you ever had a day like that?

Later that evening, when Vincent said his prayers, his mom reminded him he had to thank God for something. Vincent had to think a long time.

Finally he had something to say. This was his prayer: Dear Jesus, thank You for bandages, for medicine, for clean handkerchiefs, and for not having the snow melt yet. Amen.

# Dear Jesus,

Prayer suggestion: Have you ever had a Band-Aid day? Talk to Jesus about that time.

*Everyone who believes in Him [will]*
*not die but have eternal life.* John 3:16

# Where?

Geoffrey had a favorite winter activity. He loved to tromp around in snow. Geoffrey was outside making footprints one day when he heard a siren.

The ambulance sped by Geoffrey, then turned at the next corner. Soon the ambulance came back. The siren was blaring and the tires squealed on the snow-packed street.

Later that day Geoffrey learned more about the ambulance. Mr. Basian, Geoffrey's neighbor, had a heart attack while shoveling snow. Mr. Basian died, even though many people tried to help him.

After that winter day, Geoffrey asked many questions about people dying. He asked his mom if people could die shopping in a store. He asked his sister if someone could die riding a tractor. He asked his teacher if you could die in an ambulance.

People can die anywhere. But Geoffrey's mom told him the best thing: If you love Jesus, it doesn't matter where you die because you will go to the same wonderful heaven to live with Jesus.

# Dear Jesus,

Prayer suggestion: Talk to Jesus about someone dying.

*If you refuse good advice, you are asking for trouble.* Proverbs 13:13

# An Easy Way?

Kareem looked outside. The world was white. It had snowed overnight. He couldn't wait to get out to play.

"Now be careful," warned his mother. "There might be ice on the sidewalk."

"Ok, ok; just hurry. I want to get going," Kareem said impatiently as his mother tied his scarf.

Minutes later Kareem came into the house, crying.

"I fell on the ice," he sobbed.

"Well, why did you step on the ice?" his mother asked.

"The ice was in my way," Kareem said.

Kareem's trouble was right in the middle of the sidewalk. He could have spent a couple more seconds to walk on the other part of the sidewalk. But Kareem tromped right into trouble.

Sometimes it takes more time or trying a bit harder to keep out of trouble. What do you think Kareem will do the next time he sees ice in the middle of the sidewalk? What would you do?

# Dear Jesus,

Listening isn't always easy. And I don't always follow good advice. Help me be a better listener. Amen.

*His love is made perfect
in us.* 1 John 4:12

# Loving All Your Life

Gwen always liked this time after church. She thought it was fun to shake the pastor's hand when he was still all dressed up in "church clothes."

"I'm going to be a pastor when I grow up," Gwen's brother told Pastor Nickel today. "I want to be just like you."

Gwen listened as her brother and the pastor talked a bit. Pastor Nickel was all smiles. Gwen wondered: What could *she* say to get Pastor Nickel to smile and be happy?

"Good morning, Gwen," said Pastor Nickel. "How are you, today?"

"I'm going to love Jesus when I grow up," Gwen said. "I'm going to be a grocery checker at the store when I grow up, but I can still love Jesus."

"Why yes, Gwen," said Pastor Nickel with a big smile. "Even if you choose to drive a big fire truck when you grow up, you can still love Jesus."

Act out a job you might have when you grow up. When you do that job, you can show God's love, too.

# Dear Jesus,

I can do lots of things when I grow up. I love You now. I can still do that when I'm much, much older, too. Amen.

*Your Word is a lamp to guide me.*
Psalm 119:105

# *A Stormy Night*

The rain was beating against the windows. Lightning flashed. Thunder seemed to shake the whole building. Shelly was very afraid.

"Daddy, I don't like the storm," Shelly said. "I'm . . . "

Just then the lights blinked out. The electricity had gone off.

"Well, it's a good thing it's bedtime," her dad said cheerfully. "Help me look for a flashlight."

Shelly followed her dad to the closet. Then they looked in a drawer. There it was.

"Okay, Shelly, let's go find your pajamas," her dad said. As her dad held the flashlight for Shelly to brush her teeth, the light grew dimmer. (What do you think happened next?)

"We can't read a story without a flashlight," Shelly's dad said. Every night she listened to a different Bible story. But tonight her daddy couldn't read to her.

"Tonight why don't *you* tell *me* a story," her dad said.

"Oh, good," said Shelly. She thought of one of her favorite stories. Then she started telling about Daniel in the Lions' Den.

Pretend you are Shelly, now. The lights are off. You don't have a flashlight that works. Tell your favorite Bible story.

# *Dear Jesus,*

Thank You for the brightness of lights. Thank You for the coziness of the dark. Thank You for the Bible. Amen.

*There is nothing . . . that will ever
be able to separate us from the love
of God.* Romans 8:38–39

# *Surprises*

There are lots of surprises at Kevin's house.

Kevin's mom is surprised at all the things he leaves on the floor. (Is someone at your house surprised at what you forget to put away?)

Kevin's dad was surprised the other day when he saw how his pictures had turned out. He thought the photos would be great! They weren't.

Grandma was very surprised how fast the spinach cooked for supper. And Kevin?

Kevin is often surprised that Jesus still loves him. Sometimes Kevin forgets to be kind—but Jesus still loves him. Sometimes Kevin forgets loving words—but Jesus still loves him. Sometimes Kevin doesn't even say "I'm sorry" when he does something wrong—but Jesus still loves him.

Jesus forgives Kevin and continues to love him. Jesus forgives each of us and continues to love us, too. Are you surprised?

# *Dear Jesus,*

Thank You for surprising me with Your love and Your love and Your love. Amen.

*All the wild birds are Mine.*
Psalm 50:11

# *Feed the Birds*

"Whew, it's cold out there," said Timothy's father. He shook loose snow off his coat. He banged his boots. Little water puddles formed on the boot rack from melting snow.

"Why do you bother to fill the bird feeder when it's so cold?" Timothy asked. "Can't the birds wait till it's warmer?"

"Well, Son, my father used to feed the birds just like I do now," Timothy's dad explained. "Your grandpa always used to say that God tells some of the birds to fly to warmer places in winter. Others don't migrate.

"My dad also said God always reminded him to take care of the birds just like God took care of him," Timothy's dad said. "That's a nice idea, so that's why I feed the birds even when it's below zero outside."

"Maybe I'll tell my little boy the same story when I grow up," said Timothy. "But I'll always remember to feed the birds."

# *Dear Jesus,*

Thank You for taking care of me when the weather is cold. I love You, Jesus. Amen.

*Jesus . . . saw a very poor widow*
*dropping in two little copper coins.*
Luke 21:1–4

# Counting Pennies

Jo loved Saturday nights. That was when she got to count the week's pennies.

There was a little cup on the kitchen counter at Jo's house. If daddy found any pennies in his pockets during the week, he'd put them into the cup. On Saturday nights Jo got to look through her mother's purse for pennies. Jo would put any that she found into the penny cup. Sometimes Jo even added her own pennies. Jo had found a couple on the ground in the past few months.

On some Saturdays the penny cup was almost empty. Other weeks the penny cup was really heavy. (How many pennies do you think Jo will count this Saturday night?)

There's a special reason Jo counts pennies at the end of the week. After she counts them, she puts them into her purse. Then she takes them to church with her on Sunday morning.

Jo loves Sunday mornings, too. She feels so good putting the coins into the special bank at church. Jo thinks of the children who might hear about Jesus, just because of her penny cup.

Do you have a penny cup in your kitchen?

# Dear Jesus,

I am working to share my toys. Help me also share my money. Amen.

*Children, it is your
Christian duty to obey your
parents.* Ephesians 6:1–4

## *Mommy's Hard Day*

"Good night, Joyce," Mommy said as she clicked out the light.

Joyce's mom waited to hear, "Good night, Mommy; I love you," but Joyce didn't say anything. Her mother just sighed. It had been a long, hard day. "Joyce must still be upset she had to go to bed early," her mother thought out loud.

Joyce's mother went to the kitchen. Her feet hurt. The sink was full of dirty dishes. She still had to pack the lunches for school and work tomorrow. But Joyce's mom just sat and thought.

She didn't like it when Joyce disobeyed. Joyce knew the rules, but today she just didn't pay much attention.

Later that night, Joyce's mother prayed to Jesus. This was her prayer:

Dear Lord, help me be a good parent. Give me patience. Help Joyce be an obedient child. Help Joyce show me love. Amen.

How do you show love to your parents?

## *Dear Jesus,*

Prayer suggestion: Talk to Jesus about loving and obeying your parents.

*Since you were a child, you*
*have known the Holy Scriptures.*
2 Timothy 3:15–17

# A Winter Vacation

What fun! Kirk and his dad were going on a winter vacation. It was only for one night. It was only to a hotel in the next town. But it was still exciting!

Kirk opened his backpack. First he put in something he would need tonight. (What do you think he packed?)

Then he added something he'd use in his mouth, but he wouldn't eat. (What could that be?)

Next he added a few toys. (What toys would you pack for a trip?)

Now Kirk was ready. "Here I am, Dad," Kirk said. His dad was still packing. Kirk asked, "Why are you taking a Bible? We'll be back in time for church."

"That's one of the things I do every day, Kirk," said his dad. "Long after you are asleep, I read the Bible. But tonight you can sit up with me. I'll read, and then we can talk about what I read from the Bible."

Who reads the Bible at your house?

# Dear Jesus,

Help me make Your teachings part of my life every day. Amen.

*Love comes from God.*
1 John 4:7

# *It's Coming!*

Valentine's Day is almost here! Let's play a word game today. Finish the sentences with whatever you think of:

A valentine usually says, _____ .
Getting a valentine makes me _____ .
I hope that _____ .
People who send valentines _____ .
I know who loves me every day of the year:

_____ .

Happy Valentine's Day to you!

# *Dear Jesus,*

Thank You for loving me. Amen.

*We . . . have life through Him.* 1 John 4:9–10

# *Introducing Me!*

If a new child moves into your neighborhood, how do you introduce yourself?

When a child comes to school for the first time, what do you say about yourself?

"I'm me" is how some children introduce themselves. You might choose to say your name, where you live, or tell what you like to do. Maybe you would tell someone about your favorite books or toys.

You know all about you. But what do you know about Jesus? How would you introduce Jesus to a friend?

# *Dear Jesus,*

Sometimes I am afraid to tell my friends about You. Help me to remember that You will always love me. Amen.

*We should love one another.*
1 John 4:11

# Love Day

This was almost like Christmas, thought Erin. There was mail—lots of it! And some envelopes were even addressed to Erin Shannon!

Erin was having wonderful days this month. She loved to send valentines. She also loved to get valentines.

Erin had some favorite cards. She enjoyed those with jokes. She liked to look at valentines that were colored bright pink. It was especially fun to open cards she knew were made by her friends.

At bedtime this was Erin's prayer: Dear Jesus, thank You for giving so many people to love me. I'm glad to have valentines to send to special people, too. Thanks too, Jesus, for loving me all year 'round, not just on Valentine's Day. Good night, Jesus.

# Dear Jesus,

Prayer suggestion: Use Erin's prayer as your own.

*We have heard of your faith
in Christ Jesus.* Colossians 1:1–4

# St. Valentine's Day

Deanna was puzzled. She had been waiting and waiting for Valentine's Day. But her teacher said it was going to be *Saint* Valentine's Day.

"Mommy, what's a saint?" Deanna asked when she got home.

"Saints are those who believe that Jesus died for them," her mother answered. "You are a saint, because you are a part of God's church."

"So I'm St. Deanna?"

"Yes, I guess you could say that," laughed her mother.

"Well, then, who is St. Valentine?"

"St. Valentine was a pastor who died many years ago," her mother said. "February 14 is the day on which he died. People don't know much about him, but we do know that February 14 is the day we think of those who love us and whom we love."

"Well, then, you can just call it St. Deanna's Day and give me a valentine, anyway," said Deanna.

# Dear Jesus,

Prayer suggestion: Who are some people you love? Thank God for them now.

*I will give you life as your*
*prize of victory.* Revelation 2:10c

# St. Valentine's Day, Again!

Deanna had a puzzled look again. She had been thinking about what her mother had said.

Deanna remembered that St. Valentine was a pastor a long time ago. February 14 was the day he died. But she couldn't figure out why a sad day—when he died—became a holiday.

"Mommy, why isn't Valentine's Day on that old pastor's birthday?" asked Deanna. "It doesn't seem right to be so happy remembering somebody's 'dead' day!"

Deanna's mom didn't know the answer to that question. She called the library and, later that day, learned the answer:

Years ago, friends would remember the day a person died as a happy time. They celebrated that person's *heavenly birthday*, the day they went to live with Jesus.

Do you think that was a good idea?

# Dear Jesus,

Some things I just don't understand. Thank You for helping me learn new things. Amen.

*Let us be happy.*
Psalm 118:24

# Nothing Special?

"There's nothing to do," said Irene.

"Go outside and play. It's a beautiful winter day," said Grandpa.

"I don't have anything new to play with," said Irene.

"The sun is shining. Just walk around and soak up the warmth," her mother suggested.

"I'm bored," said Irene. "Watch the clouds drift by like you do in summer," said Grandma.

What else could Irene do?

What did you do today?

# Dear Jesus,

Today is another day. A regular day. A winter day. Help me to see the many things I can do to stay happy and busy and to do good. Amen.

*She spent all her time doing good.* Acts 9:36–42

# *Wear Jesus*

Juanita dashed into the house. She ran straight to her room. Where was the jewelry box? (Pretend to help Juanita look. Pull open a drawer—no, it's not there. Now look another place. Where will you pretend to look now? Oops, it's not there.)

Here. She found it. Juanita looked through everything in the box until there, at the bottom in a corner under the hair barrettes, she found it—her necklace with a cross.

Juanita put it on and ran to show her aunt. "Look, Aunt Mary; now everybody will know Jesus loves me," Juanita said proudly.

"Oh, Juanita," her aunt laughed. "You don't have to wear a cross for people to know you're a Christian. Everybody can tell you love Jesus just by watching you!"

Juanita looked puzzled.

"When you show kindness, you are acting like Jesus wants you to," said Aunt Mary. "Remember that day we helped someone across the street? We were showing Christian love."

"Oh, I get it," Juanita said. "When we took valentines that said 'Jesus loves you' to the nursing home, it was the same as wearing a cross."

How do you show people you are Jesus' child?

# *Dear Jesus,*

I show people I am Your child by doing some kind things. Maybe I could also show people I am Your child by _____ _____ . Amen.

*My help will come from the Lord.* Psalm 121

# *A Fire*

Lauren and her family were away from home on a vacation. They were having a wonderful time at the beach.

Then the phone rang in the hotel room. A friend from home called to say that Lauren's house had burned down. Lauren and her family got onto an airplane and flew home. They learned about the terrible explosion that had started fires everywhere in the house. Firefighters told them that anyone who had been in the house would have died or have been terribly hurt.

Lauren didn't have any toys to play with. Her clothes that hadn't burned smelled terribly smoky.

That night, when Lauren went to bed at a friend's house, her mother thanked God. She was very grateful everyone was safe. No one had been hurt.

This is a true story. Lauren is a friend of mine. The day after the fire I thanked God for protecting my friends.

# *Dear Jesus,*

Prayer suggestions: Think of a time when God has protected you or someone you know from danger. Can you thank God now for His help?

*Everyone who asks will*
*receive.* Luke 11:9–10

# Have a Problem?

Some children were talking about problems they had. Let's listen:

"If you don't want to go to swimming lessons and the parent says you have to, that's a problem," said Jordan.

"If your dad orders a hamburger instead of a cheeseburger, that's a problem," said Devon.

Act out some problems. Pretend you are sitting on a chair that is too small. What happens? If you fell off, that's a problem!

Pretend you can't get your seatbelt fastened in the car. What will you do?

There are different ways to solve problems. You can talk to people; sometimes that helps. You can think about things all by yourself. You can talk to Jesus about problems, too. He will always listen to how you feel.

# Dear Jesus,

Sometimes I have problems. I can ask these people for help:

_____ .

I know I can also talk to You about my problems, and You'll listen. Amen.

*It was while we were still*
*sinners that Christ died for us!*
Romans 5:6–8

# A February Surprise

Put your hands over your eyes—no peeking, now. Take off your hands and say, "Surprise! Surprise!" Was that fun?

Surprise! Surprise! That's what the last day of February says to us.

In some years February has 28 days; in other years February has 29 days. Go to a calendar in your house. How many days does February have this year? Surprise!

# Dear Jesus,

Thank You for always surprising us at the end of February. I'm not surprised, though, that You love me. I know I'm Your child. If I could surprise You with something extra-special, I would _____
_____ . Amen.

*The Lord does not let
us forget His wonderful actions.*
Psalm 111:4

# A Late Valentine

Brian loved to get the mail. It was always exciting to open up the mailbox and reach inside. Today there was a letter for him! That was especially fun.

He opened up the envelope. Someone had sent him a valentine.

"Mommy, look what I got!" Brian said. "Did somebody miss Valentine's Day?"

His mother glanced at the card with the big red heart. It was definitely a valentine. She read the note inside.

"It's from Uncle Art," Brian's mother explained. "He was in the hospital last month and didn't get to mail this on time. How nice he remembered you!"

Brian sat down to write a thank-you card and a get-well card to Uncle Art. What do you think Brian said to his uncle?

# Dear Jesus,

Thank You for giving me people who love me. Thank You for always remembering to love me, too. Amen.

*I love you just as the*
*Father loves Me.*
John 15:9

# *Bored?*

"I'm bored," Nicole said to no one in particular.

"I'm bored," Nicole told her aunt.

"I'm bored," Nicole told her brother.

Then Nicole was quiet. She had found something to do. What do you think Nicole was doing?

Nicole was thinking of all the people who loved her. Whom do you think she thought about?

Then Nicole smiled to herself. She was thinking about someone very special. She talked to this person every day but had never met Him. Her aunt read stories about this person from the Bible. Nicole learned about this person at Sunday school. The best thing about this person was that He always loved Nicole, no matter what she did. Whom was Nicole smiling about?

# *Dear Jesus,*

Thank You for being You. Amen.

*The message about Christ's death on
the cross . . .*
1 Corinthians 1:18

# Signs Without Words

Stephen walked home slowly. It was such a lovely spring day for looking around!

A construction worker was just putting up some flags around his neighbor's stairs. The worker looked up as Stephen walked by.

"These flags will keep people off the new steps," the worker explained. "The flags say 'Keep off.' "

"But I don't see any words," answered Stephen.

"Even your little friends will know what these flags mean," the worker explained. "Why, sonny, you just look around at all the signs without words in your neighborhood."

Stephen did look around. Sawhorses blocked off the next street. The street was being oiled. The sawhorses said "Keep away."

Stephen looked around some more. A cross peeked out from the still bare trees. What did the cross tell Stephen?

Stephen decided to act out his own signs without words. First, he pretended to tell someone to be quiet. (How would you do that?) Then he pretended to be a police officer signaling cars to stop. (Now try that.)

What other signs can you act out without words?

# Dear Jesus,

I see signs of Your love all around. You give people who take care of me and love me. Thank You for the signs of love I see this spring. Amen.

*God has forgiven you through*
*Christ.* Ephesians 4:32

# What If?

Here is a word game to play. Put on your imagination hat.

What if it snowed chocolate candy?
What if the water turned to lemonade?
What if elephants lived in trees?

Can you think of a word riddle? "What if" is a lot of fun to play with friends. But we don't have to play "What if?" with Jesus. We never have to ask, "What if Jesus loved me?" We never need to ask, "What if Jesus forgave me?"

We know He loves us. We know He forgives us. That's no fooling!

# Dear Jesus,

Thank You for Your love. I love You. Thank You for forgiving me. I try to forgive others. Amen.

---

*I am the Good Shepherd.*
John 10:14–16

# Pets

Lacey's class at church was talking about animals. The children were taking turns telling about their pets.

"We buy food for my rabbit," Jon said. "Snowy also likes peelings from the carrots and pieces of lettuce."

"My guinea pig eats some of that stuff, too," Zabelle added.

It was almost Lacey's turn. She didn't know what to say. There weren't any pets at Lacey's house right now. Her daddy was allergic to dogs and cats. Lacey's sister had some fish one time, but they died. Even the snail died! What would Lacey say?

It was Lacey's turn.

"I don't have a pet," she said. "But I *am* a pet. I am Jesus' little lamb. Jesus takes care of me just like everybody else takes care of their pets!" Lacey said.

What do you think of Lacey's answer?

# Dear Jesus,

I like feeling like a little lamb. I know You take care of me—just as You are my Shepherd. That makes me feel safe. Amen.

*Intelligent people are always*
*eager and ready to learn.*
Proverbs 18:15

# Sharing a Dustpan

Uncle Ken was sweeping. Ryan was playing cars. It was a quiet day.

"Where did the dustpan go?" Uncle Ken asked.

"I don't know," said Ryan. He was drawing a road for his cars on a big piece of cardboard.

Uncle Ken kept walking around looking for the dustpan. It was red. He should have been able to see it, but he couldn't find it.

"Ryan, I've got to get this cleaned up before your brother gets home," Uncle Ken said. "Could you help me?"

"Sure," said Ryan. "I just need to draw one more road."

"That's just it," said Uncle Ken. "I'd like to borrow your cardboard. I could use that for a dustpan."

"But I don't want a dirty road for the cars," said Ryan.

Uncle Ken and Ryan both waited quietly. They were each thinking. (How could they solve the problem?)

Then Ryan had an idea.

"Look, I don't need the whole cardboard," said Ryan. "You can rip off a piece for a dustpan."

How do you think Ryan felt about his solution? How do you feel after solving a problem?

# Dear Jesus,

Thank You for giving me a brain so I can think. I get all kinds of ideas. I think about You, too, as my Savior. Amen.

*He listens to my prayers.*
Psalm 116:1–2

# It's Pretzel Day!

Valerie looked out the window. Another gloomy day. The sun hadn't peeked through the thick clouds for a long time. Valerie's mother, though, bustled around the kitchen happily. "It's pretzel day," she said with a smile.

"Pretzel day?" Valerie asked.

"During this time before Easter we do different things to remember how important Jesus is to us," her mother explained. "Let me tell you about pretzels and praying."

"Fold your hands, Valerie, as though you were praying," her mother said. (Do that with Valerie.)

"Now show me another way you can pray." (Kneel down the way Valerie did.)

"Now cross your arms in front of you," her mother said. (Do that with Valerie.)

"Long ago that's how people prayed to God," her mother explained.

"Some people bake rolls with crosses to remind them of Jesus dying on the cross, but we'll make pretzels. That will remind us of the people who prayed to God with their arms crossed, just like a big pretzel."

# Dear Jesus,

Thank You for this time before Easter. Amen.

*The clouds that bring rain in the springtime—life is there.*
Proverbs 16:15

# It's Dropping!

One minute Karen was playing happily outside. Just a moment later she dashed into the house.

"It's dropping outside, Mommy," she said.

"Why Karen, what's dropping?"

"The rain started. It's raining again," Karen said. "Why can't I go out to play?"

"Soon the grass will start to green," said her mother. "The flowers will bud. But those plants need rain to grow."

"Our basement doesn't need rain to grow," said Karen. "I bet my toy shelf will get all wet again."

"Lots of rain is part of spring," her mother reminded Karen. "There are lots of things you like about spring."

Karen thought a minute. What good things about spring do you think Karen mentioned?

# Dear Jesus,

Thank You for the seasons. Every time of year is different. I like some seasons better. I know my favorite season will always come back again next year! Thanks, Jesus. Amen.

*I will sing with joy
because of You.* Psalm 9:1–2

# Don't Climb the Flowers!

Anika was getting ready to play at a friend's house.

"Now be polite," her mother said. "Don't climb any trees. You aren't wearing slacks today."

"I won't climb," said Anika. "Connie doesn't have any trees, and the flowers aren't big enough!"

Anika and her mother both laughed.

What fun to laugh and play. What fun did you have today?

# Dear Jesus,

Prayer suggestion: Share some of your good times with Jesus.

*So the One who came down is the
same One who went up.*
Ephesians 4:10

# Zebras and Children

What does a zebra look like?

If you said a zebra is an animal with black and white stripes, you're right.

Here's a harder question: What does a baby zebra look like?

If you said a baby zebra is smaller than an adult zebra, you're right! But a baby zebra has *brown* and white stripes! As a zebra grows up, the brown stripes change to black.

We change, too, as we grow. If you started using this book two months ago, you've grown since then.

What is one new thing you've learned recently? Have you visited a new place? Have you met a new person? Have you heard a new Bible story?

There are many ways to grow. However you grow and change, you'll still be you. And that's good!

# Dear Jesus,

Thank You for helping me grow up. Amen.

*My word is like the snow*
*and the rain.* Isaiah 55:10–11

# Upside Down, Inside Out

Think of all the things you can remember about the story of Noah. Or, ask someone to read to you about Noah and the big flood in the Bible, Genesis 6:9—9:17.

Now, here's a question: If Noah had been given some umbrellas, how would he have used them?

Would he have turned the umbrellas upside down and used them for little boats?

Would he have stuck the umbrellas into elephants' trunks to protect the smaller animals as they marched into the ark?

What do you think?

# Dear Jesus,

Sometimes I get tired of rain in the spring, but I usually still like umbrellas. Thank You for giving me things to keep me dry. Amen.

*You caused abundant rain
to fall.* Psalm 68:9

# Where Is Spring?

Shane looked glumly out the window. It was still raining! After all the rain already this spring, it was raining again. He'd never get outside to play, Shane thought.

"Where is spring, anyway?" Shane asked his dad.

His dad looked up and then walked to a window. "I'll tell you what, Son. Let's go out and find spring. We'll get a couple of umbrellas, put on some boots, and be all set," he said.

Shane and his dad got ready quickly. It wasn't very cold outside, and a walk in the rain was lots better than sitting in the house.

"First we need to smell spring," Dad said with a smile.

"Oh, that's easy," said Shane. "I can smell the dampness already." (Can you smell spring outside your house?)

"Now we need to listen for spring," said Dad.

"Oh, that's easy, too," Shane laughed. "Can't you hear the little raindrops on the umbrellas?" (Can you hear a sign of spring outside your window?)

Shane's dad then asked him to reach out and feel spring. What feels like spring to you? (Can you take a spring walk like Shane did?)

# Dear Jesus,

Thank You for spring. I especially like _____
_____ . Amen.

*We are like clay, and You
are like the potter.* Isaiah 64:8

# *Play-Dough Pretending*

Pretend you have some clay or Play-Dough on a table in front of you.

Roll it around (just pretend, of course) to get it warm and squishy.
Now shape something that makes you smile. Tell what you made.
Make something that is square. What did you make?
Make something that moves.
Make the face of someone who loves you.

# *Dear Jesus,*

Thank You for letting me imagine and pretend. Amen.

*Mary remembered all these things and*
*thought deeply about them.*
Luke 2:19

# *I Need Christmas*

"When is Christmas?" Christy asked her dad.

"It's only March, Christy," her dad answered. "Christmas is nine months away."

"I need Christmas now" Christy said. "I want the pretty lights and my big red stocking. Mostly I want the feelings."

"The feelings?" her dad asked.

"You know, Daddy—when the air is cuddly and huggy," she said. Christy's dad came over and hugged her.

"I know what you mean," he said. "The feeling of love that is so strong around Jesus' birthday. But we can have at least some of that feeling any time of year, when we think about how much Jesus loves us and when we love one another."

# *Dear Jesus,*

At Christmas everybody seems to love everybody else. Help me feel like Christmas every time I remember that You love me. Amen.

*Flowers will bloom in the wastelands.* Isaiah 35:1–2

# Happy Spring!

"Good morning," said Mother as she came into the bedroom. "We begin a new season today. Happy spring, Alexis!"

Alexis jumped out of bed and ran to the window. The trees still looked bare. The grass was still brownish, and there wasn't a flower anywhere.

"It doesn't look like spring," Alexis said. "It doesn't look any different than yesterday."

"Spring is like the earth's birthday," her mother explained. "Do you feel any different the day after your birthday?"

"Well, no," replied Alexis. "I'm sorry things don't look bright and happy like spring should look today. But I can still say, 'Happy Birthday, Earth!' "

# Dear Jesus,

Thank You for the promise of newness that we have with spring. Buds promise flowers, and eggs in nests mean baby birds will soon be born. Thank You for this special season. Amen.

*[Sent] to be . . . Savior.*
John 3:17

# Looking Ahead

"What are you going to do when you grow up?" Has anyone ever asked you that question?

When you are older you might have a job to help children who are sick. You might cook for people. You might fix streetlights. What else could you do?

When Jesus was older, He died on the cross for us. He is our Savior. His job was to show how much God loves us and forgives us.

You might do many different things when you grow up. You might be a mother, an aunt, and a computer programmer—all at the same time!

When Jesus grew up, He was a preacher and a teacher. But most of all, Jesus is our Savior.

# Dear Jesus,

I can call You my Friend. I can call You my Shepherd. Most of all, though, You are my Savior. Amen.

*It is I. Don't be afraid.*
Mark 6:45–51

# *Scary Things*

Sumiko was watching TV when a flashing dot appeared at the bottom of the screen. Then an announcer broke into the program. The announcer warned of bad weather coming to the area.

Sumiko was scared. She ran straight into the kitchen, calling, "Grandma, Grandma! They said there's a tornado watching. I'm so scared."

"It's probably a tornado watch, Sumiko," Grandma answered. "That means there might be a bad windstorm. But come here and let me hug you."

Sumiko settled into her grandma's arms. It wasn't so scary, now. (Can someone hug you now, too? That feels so good!)

Have you ever been afraid of some type of weather? What are some things that scare you?

Sumiko felt better when her grandma hugged her. Sumiko wasn't as afraid. God gives us people to help care for us. (Draw a picture of someone who takes care of you.)

# *Dear Jesus,*

Prayer suggestion: Talk to Jesus about what worries you. Then thank Him for giving you people who give you hugs.

*A Samaritan . . . came upon
the man.* Luke 10:30–35

# Bumps and Itches

Kara didn't feel good. Her head hurt. Little bumps popped up on her tummy. She itched. (Do you know what was wrong with Kara? She had chicken pox.)

Kara didn't sleep well. Kara's grandma got up at night to give her a drink.

Kara kept itching. Kara's daddy put on some lotion.

Kara was crabby. Kara's sister made her a funny picture.

Do you know what happened? Kara started getting better.

The chicken pox didn't itch so much. Her head didn't hurt. Kara wasn't nearly as crabby.

When Kara went to bed the next night, she said this prayer:

Dear God: I hate the chicken pox, but thank You for taking care of me. Amen.

Can you think of how God took care of Kara?

When we are hurt or sick or scared, God sends people to help us. God took care of Kara by giving her people to help her.

What people has God given you to help you?

# Dear Jesus,

Thank You for people who help when I'm sick, people like Dr. _____ . Thank You for someone to help my teeth stay healthy, like Dr. _____ . Amen.

*Whoever believes in Me will live,*
*even though he dies.* John 11:25–27

## *No Wrinkles in Heaven*

Ileana was sitting in one of her favorite places in the whole world: her grandmother's lap. Ileana always felt so safe here, so cozy and so happy.

But today Ileana was worried. She looked into her grandmother's face. All those wrinkles on Grandma's face and neck must mean that she was getting old, Ileana thought. That worried Ileana.

"Grandma, I've been thinking," Ileana said. "I'm scared you're going to die."

"Does that worry you, Ileana?" Grandma asked.

"Yes, 'cause then I'll miss you, and you won't be here to cuddle me, and we won't sit and talk after you die," Ileana said in one breath.

Grandma smiled and didn't look at all upset.

"You know I'll die someday," Grandma said. "And I will miss you. But I'm not worried about dying."

"You aren't?" Ileana asked. She couldn't understand that.

"I'll be with Jesus after I die," Grandma said. "And someday you'll be in heaven with Jesus and me. Maybe I won't even have all these wrinkles on my face."

How do you think Ileana felt after talking with her grandmother?

## *Dear Jesus,*

Prayer suggestion: Talk to Jesus about how you feel.

*They found the stone*
*rolled away.* Luke 24:1–9

# A Present for Easter

"Lance, why so sad today?" Grandpa asked. "Easter's coming!"

"Aw, Grandpa. Easter's no fun," said Lance. "Easter is just eggs, and I hate hard-boiled eggs."

"Well, Lance, you know you can't have all that sugar in jelly beans and candy," said Grandpa.

"Easter's a no-fun holiday," said Lance.

Then Grandpa had an idea you can try. He and Lance went outside to look for smooth rocks. They washed them off. Then Lance painted crosses on the rocks.

Lance spent the whole afternoon using crayons and markers to make Easter rocks. He couldn't wait to put them into Easter baskets.

Who can help you make Easter rocks?

# Dear Jesus,

Help me remember the real message of Easter. Amen.

*The Lord is risen indeed!*
Luke 24:28–34

# Easter Egg Cartons

"There's nothing to do now," Elliot complained.

"Why, Elliot; I just spent all morning decorating eggs with you boys," his father answered. "How can you say there's nothing to do?"

"Elliot's right, Dad," Jason said, "Easter fun is over before Easter even gets here. There's nothing left now."

His father was quiet. Then he said, "Boys, that makes me very sad. We wouldn't even have Easter if Jesus hadn't risen. That's the real meaning of Easter.

"Here; you guys each take an empty egg carton," Dad said. "This afternoon use the egg carton to make something that shows the real meaning of Easter. We'll talk about your Easter egg cartons at suppertime."

Jason and Elliot glumly picked up the cartons.

What do you think they made?

At suppertime each boy proudly brought his Easter egg carton creation. Jason had made a model of the first Easter. He had ripped apart pieces of the egg carton to make the tomb, a garden with trees, and people. He used a tissue to show the tomb where Jesus had been laid.

What do you think Elliot brought?

Ask your parent for an empty egg carton. Use your carton to make what you think Elliot did with his Easter egg carton.

# Dear Jesus,

I know You are the real reason for Easter. Sometimes, with the Easter eggs and candies, I forget that. Please help me to remember Your empty tomb. Amen.

*He has been raised from death.*
Matthew 28:1–7

## Some Easter Fun

Here's an Eastertime game you can play. It goes like this:

When I think of Easter, I think of bunnies.
*Can you do something rabbits do?*

When I think of Easter, I think of eggs.
*Can you pretend to be a little chick hatching?*

When I think of Easter, I think of flowers.
*Can you pretend to grow from a seed into a plant?*

When I think of Easter, I think of Jesus.
*Now what can you do?*

## Dear Jesus,

I love so much about Eastertime. I like to hear about the first Easter.
That story makes me feel _____ . Amen.

*So they entered the tomb, where they
saw a young man . . . wearing a
white robe.* Mark 16:1–8

# *Playing Easter*

"Heather, what are you doing?" her mother said.

"I'm playing Easter," Heather answered. "See? Don't I look like an angel?"

Her mother smiled at Heather's costume.

(What would you wear to dress as an angel?)

"I see you found a paper plate for a halo," her mother said. "And that clean sheet from the wash basket does make a nice gown. But Heather, why did you turn the clothes basket upsidedown?"

"That's the tomb," Heather said happily. "And see, it's empty. Jesus has already jumped out!"

Was Heather right about Easter? Can you act out the story of Easter now?

# *Dear Jesus,*

Thank You for the first Easter. Thank You for this Easter. Amen.

*Then she . . . saw Jesus standing
there.* John 20:11–18

# Another Easter?

Ashley loved Eastertime. Unpacking the box of Easter baskets was such fun! And all the pretend grass made a pretty sight inside the baskets. She even got to eat a few candy eggs when she and her mommy fixed little baskets to give to friends. Yes, Easter was a favorite time of year for Ashley.

What do you like about Easter? Can you think of something special you get to eat at Easter? Can you think of what you might wear on Easter?

There was one thing Ashley didn't understand about Easter. Let's listen as she talks with her mommy:

"I thought we had Easter last year, Mommy," Ashley said.

"Well, of course we had Easter last year, Ashley," her mother replied. "We even used the same baskets."

"How can we have Easter again?" Ashley asked. "Does Jesus keep dying and rising every year?"

Ashley's mother answered her question this way: "Jesus died and rose on the first Easter. We just remember that first Easter every year. If Jesus hadn't risen, we wouldn't even have an Easter."

Do you have any questions about Easter?

# Dear Jesus,

I like the brightness and happy feeling of Easter. Please help me keep that Easter feeling inside me. Amen.

*Mary Magdalene went to the tomb.*
John 20:1–10

# Olden Day Easters

"Grandpa, what was Easter like in the olden days when you were little?" Victoria asked.

"Well, Victoria," Grandpa said, "we colored eggs in a different way. We did it like my parents did in England when they were little.

"First I carefully took a raw egg," he explained. "Then we wrapped brown onion skin around the egg and an old rag around that.

"My mother always helped tie a string around the cloth," Grandpa added. "Then the egg was boiled for about 20 minutes.

"When we unwrapped the hard-boiled egg, it was a shade of yellow or brown," Grandpa said.

"Wow, Grandpa! That really is different," Victoria said. "To make pink eggs we used rose petals," Grandpa added.

"Wow," said Victoria.

"But let me tell you, Child, " Grandpa added, "there's one thing that was the same then for me as it is for you this Easter."

What is Grandpa thinking of?

# Dear Jesus,

Some things are very different now from years ago. But I know that people went to church a long time ago just as I go to church now. And they dressed up in their best clothes on Easter Sunday, too. But the most important thing that's the same is You. You are the reason for Easter. Amen.

*He is not here;*
*He has been raised.* Luke 24:1–9

# No Easter Bunny?

Manuel had lots of fun playing with his friend, Claire. But now Manuel was running home. And Manuel was crying.

Manuel raced into the house. "Mommy, Mommy," he called.

"Oh, Mommy," Manuel came up to his mother, "Claire says there's no Easter bunny. If there's no Easter bunny, how can we have Easter?"

Manuel laid his head on his mother's lap and cried. When he calmed down, she talked to him quietly.

"Manuel, your little friend is right about one thing," his mother said. "We don't need a bunny to have Easter. We don't need chicks, or eggs, or Easter baskets. All we need is Jesus and what happened on the first Easter."

Manuel was quiet. He thought about what his mother said.

You can read about the first Easter in the Bible. Look up the story in Luke 24:1–9.

# Dear Jesus,

Easter means lots of things. Easter means eggs. Easter means springtime. Easter means _____ .

Most of all, Easter means You are alive as my Savior. Amen.

# Devotion Seven

*So He took some soil . . . and formed
all the animals and all the birds.*
Genesis 2:19

## Animal Riddles

Here are some riddles. Every answer is the name of an animal. See if
you can guess the animals.

This animal has a long neck. It
has spots. It has very long legs and
lives in Africa. Sometimes you see
this animal in the zoo. What is it?

This animal barks (but it's not a
dog). This animal eats fish (but it's
not a whale). This animal sometimes
claps its flippers in a zoo show. What
is it?

This animal looks like a pig with a hard shell. It has a long tail. It
lives in the southern part of the United States, especially in Florida and
Texas. What is it?

God made all the animals. He made giraffes, seals, and armadillos.
(Did you guess them all?) God gives us cats to pet and dogs to walk.

What animals do you like best?

## Dear Jesus,

Thank You for animals that bark like _____ .
Thank You for animals that wag their tails like _____ .
Thank You for animals that wiggle like _____ . Amen.

*God will put His angels*
*in charge of you.* Psalm 91:11–12

# Afraid of the Dark

"I get afraid at night," Yoshi said. "I think the big bad wolf will climb through the window."

"I always think there is a robber with a gun," said Yasuko. "I stay awake all night."

"I get scared, too," said Rosanne.

"Do your eyes stay open all night, Rosanne?" Yoshi asked.

"Oh, no," said Rosanne. "Mommy told me it's okay to be scared sometimes. That's when I just talk to Jesus. Sometimes I sing songs, too," said Rosanne. Sing with her:

Jesus loves me; this I know,
For the Bible tells me so.
Little ones to Him belong.
They are weak, but He is strong.
Yes! Jesus loves me! Yes! Jesus loves me!
Yes! Jesus loves me! The Bible tells me so.

Lots of children are afraid at night. Some children get scared when they walk into a dark room. Maybe even Jesus was afraid when He was a little boy.

Now, though, Jesus is ready to help you at night. You can sing to Him. You can talk to Him. He even sends someone to watch you at night. Who do you think that is?

Find the answer in the Bible. Ask someone to read Psalm 91:11–12.

# Dear Jesus,

I know Your angels watch over me. Thank You, Jesus. Amen.

*Christ died for our sins . . . He
was raised to life three days later.*
1 Corinthians 15:3–7

# *Hooray! Hooray!*

This is an action poem. Do what the words tell you:

- I want to clap my hands. I want to give a cheer.
Hooray! Hooray! Easter is here.
- I want to turn around. I want to stamp my feet.
Hooray! Hooray! Easter is neat.
- I want to tap my head. I'll wiggle an ear.
Hooray! Hooray! Easter is here.
- I want to tap my elbow. I will reach to heaven.
Hooray! Hooray! Jesus is risen.
- My body will shout. I'll tell everyone.
Hooray! Hooray! Jesus is God's Son.
- I'll hold my waist. Then I'll touch my nose.
Hooray! Hooray! Jesus Christ rose.
- I'll jump on the floor, then sit right down.
Hooray! Hooray! Jesus wears a crown.

# *Dear Jesus,*

Thank You for Easter. Amen.

*Once there was a man who*
*went out to sow grain.* Mark 4:3–8

# Planting Time

"What a great day for planting," Daddy said at breakfast. "I can't wait to spread that grass seed."

"Do you have to plant grass?" Daria asked. "I thought it just grew."

Everyone at the breakfast table laughed. Everybody laughed— except Daria's dad.

"Let's look," he said. He and Daria walked over to the window. The whole area around their new house was a sea of mud. Mud, mud, mud.

"Won't grass just grow, Daddy?" Daria asked.

"It won't grow unless we plant it," he answered. "So let's go outside and start it growing."

Daria tried to think of other plants that grew from seeds. Look outside your window. How many things do you see that grew from seeds?

# Dear Jesus,

Thank You for seeds that grow, like _____ ;
for seeds I eat, like _____ ;
for seeds that look pretty, like _____ . Amen.

*I love you.* John 15:9

# You Can't See It, but . . .

There are at least two answers to
today's riddle. See if you can
guess them.

You can't see it.
You can't touch it.
You can't taste it.
But it is everywhere.
What is it?

Did you guess air? You couldn't blow up a balloon without air. You couldn't fly your spring kite without air. But we can't see it, touch it, or taste it. We need air, though, to live.

Maybe you guessed another answer to the riddle. Did you answer "Jesus' love"? We can't see Jesus' love floating through the air; we can't reach out and grab it; we can't taste Jesus' love. But we need it to live a caring, loving life.

# Dear Jesus,

I'm glad You love me. I know I can't see You, but I feel Your love when someone is nice to me. That just happened when (*say what happened to you*). I'm glad Your love is all around me. Amen.

*You are . . . members of*
*the family of God.* Ephesians 2:19

# Just the Two of Us

Dorothy dragged her feet. It had not been a good day at school.
(What do you think made Dorothy sad?)

Dorothy's class had talked about families. Then everybody made their houses. Each child cut a window out for every member of the family. Dorothy only got to cut out two windows. (How many windows would you cut out for your family?)

"Mommy, it's not fair," Dorothy complained as she walked in the front door. "Everybody has a bigger family than we have."

Her mother listened as Dorothy explained the school project.

"Honey, a bigger family doesn't mean a better family," her mother said. Dorothy still looked sad.

Her mother thought for a while. She and Dorothy had very many good times together. They loved each other a whole lot.

"You know, Dorothy," her mother said, "you probably belong to the biggest family of all. You and I both belong to God's family, so we have everything we could want," Dorothy's mother explained. "We have the two of us when we want to just be alone, and that's nice. And when we want to feel part of a bigger family, we just have to remember we're part of God's family."

How do you think Dorothy feels now? How many windows would you cut out for your family now? Make a paper house for your family, just as Dorothy did at school.

# Dear Jesus,

Thank You for people who love me. Amen.

*Look at the birds . . . your Father*
*in heaven takes care of them.*
Matthew 6:26–27

# Why?

Jo Ellyn and Pierre watched a robin make a nest right outside the window. The bird kept coming to the nest with bits of dead grass. One day the robin flew in with a long, long string. Then the robin brought something that really surprised Jo Ellyn and Pierre.

(What do you think that was?)

Each day the children looked out the corner of the window into the nest. At first, the nest looked like a big mess. But every day, now, the nest was looking neater. The robin wiggled into the grass and twigs to make the nest fit just right.

One day the robin didn't come to the nest. Nor the next day.

The bird that had worked many days making a great nest never did come back. (What do you think happened to the bird?)

Jo Ellyn and Pierre were very disapppointed. They felt sad, too. The children never found out what happened to their friendly robin.

Have you ever wondered why something happened—and didn't get an answer? Sometimes there aren't any good answers. We don't understand everything that goes on. But God does. He has a plan for everything and everyone. God will take care of us.

# Dear Jesus,

Sometimes I don't understand everything. I know You do. I know that You will always take care of me. Amen.

*The Lord . . . is good to everyone.*
Psalm 145:8–9

# At the Airport

Julian stood with his dad and looked out the airport terminal windows. He saw all kinds of cars and trucks and wagons rolling around. This was a busy place!

Then Julian heard a motor start up. (What kind of motor could it have been?)

Next, Julian turned around. Some people in different kinds of uniforms were walking through the terminal. (What kind of work do you think those people did?)

Julian turned around quickly to look out the window again. A jumbo jet was taking off.

"Dad, how does God make airplanes fly?" Julian asked.

"God doesn't make the airplanes fly, Julian," his dad answered. "But God did give good minds to people, and some of them figured out how to make airplanes fly."

"Will I be that smart some day?" Julian asked.

"Everybody is good at some things," Dad answered.

"Like I can ride a two-wheeler?" Julian asked.

"Yes, Julian," his dad answered. "God has been very good to you."

God is good to all of us in different ways. How has God been good to you?

# Dear Jesus,

Thank You for always caring about me. Amen.

---

*Whoever loves is a child of God.*
1 John 4:7

# *Who Is It?*

Many people help care for us. God lets different people help us at different times. Answer these riddles with the name of the person who helps you:

- I sit in a special chair. The chair goes up and down. Somebody looks in my mouth. Somebody uses a little mirror to count my teeth. Who is this somebody?
- I go here to keep well. I visit this person when I am sick, too. Sometimes I get medicine from this person. I usually feel better when I leave this person. Who is this somebody?
- I go here to learn about Jesus. I sing songs and have fun. This person is always glad I come to Sunday school. Who is this person?
- I go here when my shoes are too tight. I get new shoes here. This person measures my feet. I put my foot up on a chair with a funny little ramp. Who is this somebody?

# *Dear Jesus,*

Thank You, Jesus, for the people who help You help me. Amen.

*He [God] loved us
and sent His Son.* 1 John 4:9–10

## *Shopping Time*

Let's pretend we're going shopping for food. What's the first thing you do? Act it out. Can the person reading this book guess what you do first in the store?

Now pretend to find one of your favorite foods. Can you reach it on the shelf? Is the package heavy or light? Act it out. Can the person guess what you're going to buy. Did your reader guess right?

Now it's time to check out. Where do you get the money?

We can buy many things at the grocery store. We can get all kinds of food. We can buy all sorts of things for the house. We can even buy a lot of things that aren't groceries.

There's one thing we cannot buy at a grocery store—or anywhere else. That's God's love.

We don't have to buy God's love. It's free for you. It's free for me. It's free for everyone.

## *Dear Jesus,*

Prayer suggestion: Thank God for His love.

*God looked at everything He had
made, and He was very pleased.*
Genesis 1:31

# Earth Week at Danielle's House

What a great week it had been at Danielle's house! Every Sunday in April something different was set in the middle of the kitchen table. Earlier this month the family had little Easter bunnies and chicks. Last week her brother put his favorite truck on the table. Her brother loved that.

But Danielle really liked this week. A globe sat in the middle of the table. While supper was cooking, Danielle and her brother played a game. Danielle would close her eyes and spin the globe. She would open her eyes, tell whether her finger landed on water or land, and her brother would read the name of the place. What fun!

Danielle had learned a lot. She learned that the globe looks like our earth. It is round. It spins. It is tilted sideways a bit. And, there is more water than land. (The blue color on the globe showed that.)

But Danielle didn't know the answer to one question: "How did God make the earth, Daddy?" she asked.

"I wasn't there, Danielle," her father said. "But I do know that God did make it. Let's read in the Bible about what happened."

Danielle and her father sat down. She liked hearing about the trees and the animals that God created.

You can hear about creation, too. Ask someone to read you the story in Genesis 1:1–31.

# Dear God,

Thank You
for making green things that grow, like _____ ;
for making yellow things that smell good, like _____ ;
and for making everything on Your beautiful earth. Amen.

*No one has ever seen God.*
1 John 4:12

## *Let's Play!*

Let's play a thinking game. Listen to each riddle, then answer the question. There can be many right answers.

- This person lives far away. You don't see this person very often. But when this person and you see each other, the first thing you do is hug each other. Who is this person?
- This person lives near you. You are always glad to see this person come. When this person isn't here, you wait eagerly for him. Who is this?
- You see this person a lot. This person doesn't live in your house, though. You always have fun with this person. Who is this?
- You love this person, but never hug Him. You talk to this person, and He never interrupts. This person is here and everywhere else, too. Who is this person?

## *Dear Jesus,*

I really do love You. I talk to You, too. I know You love me. Amen.

*The Lord has forgiven you.*
Colossians 3:12–13

# Somebody Knows Your Secret

Ewaldo threw down his piano books. What an awful lesson he had!

"How was piano, Ewaldo?" his mother asked.

"Horrible," Ewaldo answered. "How did Mrs. Ansley know I didn't practice? Did you tell her, Mom?"

"Oh, no," Ewaldo's mother answered. "She could just tell how well you knew your lesson."

"Well, how?" Ewaldo asked again.

"Just like the dentist knew last week that you hadn't been brushing your teeth," Ewaldo's mother said. "And just like God knows when you sneak candy to eat in bed at night."

"That's awful!" Ewaldo said angrily. "I'm going to my room! And don't come in!" Ewaldo slammed the door.

Ewaldo felt horrible. It was no use. He did lots of bad things, and he guessed that God knew about everything.

Ewaldo felt horrible—until he remembered something. Then he said this prayer:

Dear Jesus, I'm sorry I do bad things sometimes. But I just remembered that You forgive me. You still love me. You will always love me. That makes me feel much better. Amen.

# Dear Jesus,

Prayer suggestion: Pray Ewaldo's prayer as your prayer today.

*Trust in the Lord now and
forever.* Psalm 131:2–3

# Why Do I Have to Grow Up?

Timothy decided that he didn't want to grow up. When he was a baby, it was alright to suck his thumb. When he was a little boy, it was alright to suck his thumb. But now that he was growing bigger, his father had said, "No more thumb-sucking!"

Timothy had tried to stop sucking his thumb. Every time he thought about it, he pulled his thumb out of his mouth. His dad said he just didn't think about it enough. What could Timothy do?

His father said, "You'll have to wear a sock on your hand at night so you can't suck your thumb."

His grandmother said, "Get a drink of water every time you feel like sucking your thumb."

His brother said, "I'll give you a trading card every day you don't suck your thumb."

Now, you tell the end of this story.

# Dear Jesus,

It's not easy to grow up. Sometimes my new teeth hurt when they come in. Now that I'm bigger, I have to do more work. Whenever I think about the things I don't like, please help me remember the good things about growing up. Amen.

*The Lord has given us eyes
to see with.* Proverbs 20:12

# *Those Wonderful Eyes*

Andrea dragged her feet up the steps. She didn't want to go home because, as soon as she got home, she would have to get her new eyeglasses.

"Good, Andrea," her mother said. "Your new glasses are ready. Have a quick snack and let's go."

Andrea dragged into the kitchen. Her mother looked up and said, "Oh, Honey, I'm sorry you aren't happy about your new glasses. But wait till you find out how well you can see with them!"

Andrea looked up. She wasn't smiling.

"Andrea, I want you to look at this," her mother said. "What did God give you to protect your eyes?"

Andrea felt all around her eyes. (What did she feel?)

"My eyebrows?" she asked.

"That's right. They keep some dust out of your eyes," her mother said. "Now gently touch your eyelashes." (Do that with Andrea. What happens?)

"I can't help blinking," Andrea said.

"That's right," her mother said. "They automatically try to close if something is coming too close to your eyes. Now feel around your eye." (Do that with Andrea.)

"There's a bone," Andrea said.

"That's right, too," her mother said. "God made our eyes to be surrounded by things that protect our sight. I'm just so grateful you have eyes to see. And after today you'll be able to see even better!"

How do you think Andrea felt now?

# *Dear Jesus,*

I love looking at _____ . Thank You for my eyes. Amen.

*I am putting My bow in
the clouds.* Genesis 9:12–17

# I Hate Rain!

The day had been beautiful. The new grass was turning green. Some bushes were flowering. And the sun was so warm it even heated up the sand in Henry's sandbox. It had been a beautiful day—until now.

Henry dashed into the house to beat the raindrops. He didn't even know it was going to rain. The sky still looked light.

"I hate rain. I hate rain," Henry complained as he rubbed his hair dry with a towel. "Why did it rain, Mommy?"

"It rained so we could have a rainbow, Henry," his mother answered. "Come here, quickly! Look up!"

Henry looked. The colors weren't bright, but he could see a rainbow—a real rainbow.

What colors did Henry see in the rainbow? [An easy way to remember the colors of the rainbow is to know *Roy G. Biv.* Each letter of this pretend-person's name starts one of the color names: *R*ed, *O*range, *Y*ellow, *G*reen, *B*lue, *I*ndigo, *V*iolet.]

"Oh, Mommy," Henry said softly. "It's my first rainbow, my very first rainbow."

They stood and watched out the window until the rainbow was gone.

"Before bed tonight, Henry, let's read the story of the very first rainbow," his mother said. "Then, every time you're unhappy with rain, you can remember your first rainbow and the very first rainbow."

Read about God's first rainbow in the Bible.

# Dear Jesus,

Thank You for this color-filled world.

*She gave birth to
her first son.* Luke 2:7

# *Egg Talk*

Gaylord found something on the ground. It was blue and very thin. It was cracked and small. It had fallen from a nest in a tree. What did he find?

People who study birds are called ornithologists. Birds are hatched. Do you know what "hatch" means?

People don't crack open a shell and hatch. God has made a wonderful way for us to be born.

Jesus had a mother and was born in the same way as every other person. And God cared for His own Son just as He cares for us.

What did you look like after you were born? Where were you born?

Ask your parents to tell you about your birth. Then read the story of another baby's birth. You'll find that in Luke 2:1–7.

# *Dear Jesus,*

I know some animals hatch from eggs, like birds and turtles. But I didn't hatch.

I have a real mommy, just as You did when You were born. That makes me feel so special! Amen.

*His angel guards those who have*
*reverence for the Lord.* Psalm 34:7

# Voices in the Night

Betsy rolled over in bed. She was having a hard time getting to sleep on this warm night. The window in her bedroom was open, and Betsy heard many strange noises. First she heard bugs. Then she heard some birds.

Now she heard voices. Betsy crept down the stairs. No, it wasn't Daddy talking on the phone.

Betsy went back to bed. But she still heard voices. Maybe her neighbors were out in the backyard. Betsy tiptoed to the window. No one was outside.

Betsy crawled back into bed. Then she heard music, too. "So that's it!" Betsy thought. She went to sleep with a smile.

At breakfast the next morning Betsy told her father, "Daddy, I heard your angel talking to my angel last night."

Her father looked puzzled.

"I kept hearing voices," Betsy explained. "Then I heard pretty music, too. That's how I knew it was the angels talking and playing their harps."

Her father put his head back and laughed. "I was listening to a concert on the radio after you went to bed," he said. "But, perhaps you did hear angels after all."

What do you think Betsy really heard?

# Dear Jesus,

Thank You for watching over me. Thank You for sending Your angels to protect me, too. Amen.

*With them went every kind of
animal.* Genesis 7:1–16

# *"A" Is for Animal*

Gina loved the zoo. Spring at the zoo was best of all; there were lots of baby animals.

Gina liked to visit the place where lots of things crawled around. (Where in the zoo did Gina go to see these animals?)

Gina laughed when she saw other animals swing from their tails. (What animals did Gina laugh at?)

Gina raced over to see what was barking. (What did Gina run to see?)

The animals you and Gina see at the zoo are like the ones that took a boat trip a long time ago. You can read the story in the Bible. Look for Genesis 7:1–16.

What is your favorite animal at the zoo? When you talk to Jesus today, thank Him for that wonderful creature.

We know God created all the animals. Aren't you glad of that?

# *Dear Jesus,*

Thank You for animals that wiggle and those that squiggle, for animals with fur and animals that purr, and for all animals. Amen.

*God had not forgotten Noah and*
*all the animals with him in the*
*boat.* Genesis 8:1–5

# Car Wash Time

Jodie loved going through a car wash.

(Show how the big hose sprays water. Now pretend you are the soap suds. Can you show how the big, cloth arms wash a car? Now be the giant blow dryer. Great! You're ready to ride through the car wash with Jodie. Here we go.)

"Daddy, if we had a van, how would we get it washed?" Jodie asked as the hose sprayed the water.

"We'd need to go to a larger car wash," her dad said.

"If we had a pickup truck, how would we get it washed," Jodie asked. The soap suds were swishing on the windshield.

"We'd drive the pickup to a truck wash," her dad said.

"Daddy, if we had a mobile home, how would we get it washed?" Jodie asked. The big arms came over the top of the car, back and forth, back and forth.

"I guess we'd have to pay someone to wash it for us," her dad said.

Now it was time for the giant blowers to dry their car. (Can you blow the car dry?)

Jodie had one more question. Can you answer it?

"Daddy, how did Noah keep the ark clean? It wouldn't fit in a car wash."

What would you tell Jodie?

# Dear Jesus,

Thank You for giving us clean water. We wash our car. We wash our clothes. We wash me. We _____. Help us use water wisely. Amen.

*Clouds that bring rain in
the springtime—life is there.*
Proverbs 16:15

# A Spring Walk

Let's take an imaginary walk today. We're going to look for signs of spring.

Let's look in the grass first. What signs of spring can you find?

Now let's look up. How many signs of spring can you see? Is one of those spring things moving?

Here's a hard question: Can you find signs of spring on the sidewalk? Look for things that crawl. Can you think of any? Sometimes there are cracks in the sidewalk; are there any signs of spring there?

In spring God's world wakes up from a winter rest. How do you feel in spring?

# Dear Jesus,

Thank You for spring. I especially like _____
_____ . Amen.

*The Lord God planted
a garden in Eden.* Genesis 2:8–9

## It's Cleaning Day

Look around where you are sitting. Do you see any dust? Is some hiding behind a chair? under a bed? on the chair bottom?

Peggy's house has a lot of dust. She is helping her father clean. Let's listen as they talk:

"Daddy, why is it dusty already?" Peggy asks. "We did the same cleaning last week."

"Peggy, there's dust almost everywhere," her father answers. "Now that the weather is warm, the wind blows dust into the rooms from outside."

"Let's close the windows," Peggy suggests.

"That won't help much," her father says. "You even make some of the stuff we vacuum up. See? Here's a piece of hair. And last week we found a fingernail. And sometimes your clothes leaves bits of threads or lint."

Peggy is thinking about what her father said. She thinks of one place where there wasn't any dust. (What place do you think she is thinking of?)

Peggy is thinking about the garden God created for the first people on earth.

"I'll bet they didn't have cleaning day in the Garden of Eden," Peggy says. (Do you think Peggy is right?)

## Dear Jesus,

Cleaning up isn't always much fun. Help me be cheerful when I work. Amen.

*Happy are those who . . .*
*die in . . . the Lord.*
Revelation 14:13

# Growing Bigger, Growing Smaller

"Daddy, I need to tell you something," Otto whispered. "Granny's shrinking."

"That's possible, Otto," his dad said. "As your great-grandmother has grown older, her body has changed in different ways. It might look like she's shrinking."

"Pretty soon I'll be as tall as she is," Otto said.

"Yes," his father smiled. "You are a growing boy."

Otto thought his great-grandma looked even smaller the next time he visited. But maybe, just maybe, he had grown, too.

"Granny," Otto said. "I'll love you even if you get smaller."

"Otto," said Granny. "I'll love you even if you get bigger."

Otto and Granny both smiled. Otto wondered, though, would he be taller than Granny when they got to heaven? What do you think?

# Dear Jesus,

I wonder a lot about heaven. Will I be the same as I am now? Will I have the same friends? I wish I could know more about heaven, but I guess I'll just find out when I get there. Thanks for listening. Amen.

*God made peace through*
*His Son's . . . death on the cross.*
Colossians 1:20

# *Shadow Play*

"Mommy, can I have a drink of water?" Sally asked.

"Ok; go downstairs and get one," said her mother. "But then it's bedtime, for sure."

"I'm afraid to go down by myself," said Sally.

"Why?" her mother asked. "I need to tuck Patrick in bed, so I can't go down with you."

"I'm afraid of the shadows," Sally explained. "They look so scary on the walls."

"Wait a minute," her mother said with a sigh. "I'll go down with you."

A few minutes later, as they stood at the top of the steps, Mother said to Sally, "Make a cross with your fingers. Hold them up like this to block out the light as you go down the stairs. What looks like it's going with you?"

"It looks like a cross walking downstairs!" Sally said.

"You know that Jesus is always watching over you," her mother said. "If you're ever afraid in the dark, just make your fingers in the shape of the cross of Jesus. That will help remind you that you'll never be alone."

Turn on a light in your room now. Go very close to the wall. Now make a cross with your fingers like Sally did. Walk along the wall like that. You, too, can always take a reminder of Jesus along with you.

# *Dear Jesus,*

Even though I might be all alone, I don't have to be lonely. I know that You are always with me. Amen.

*Lord, You have made
so many things!* Psalm 104:10–28

# Be Alive!

Make some actions for this poem.
Stand up, now. Ready? Here we go:

The grass is growing;
It soon will need mowing.

The clouds are moving fast;
How long will the sunshine last?

The wind is starting to blow.
Look! Watch that rabbit go.

I hear the birdies calling.
Now some rain is falling.

God is caring for our earth.
It's spring. The time of new birth.

Chickens hatch. Puppies are born.
Farmers plant wheat, oats, and corn.

Thank You, Jesus, for giving us spring.
Thank You, Jesus, is what I want to sing.

# Dear Jesus,

Prayer suggestion: Pray by singing a song for Jesus.

*Christ . . . lives in me.*
Galatians 2:20

# Thumbs Up!

Let's play a game. If something is good, put your thumbs up. If the sentence is not good, point your thumbs down. Practice it: thumbs up; now thumbs down.

Let's start:

- Sometimes I don't share my toys.
- I fussed when I set the table for dinner.
- I fussed when I couldn't do what I wanted to do.
- I helped rake up the grass.
- I cleaned up my room.
- I brushed my teeth without being told.
- I put away my toys.
- I am playing this game.

Because you are Jesus' child, playing this game is "thumbs up." That's because you know how Jesus wants you to act. Everybody makes mistakes (that's thumbs-down time), but Jesus always forgives us (and that's thumbs up).

When you're making a decision—to act the way you know is right, or to do something wrong—remember "thumbs up." You are Jesus' child, and He will help you do what is right.

# Dear Jesus,

I am Your child. I am glad! Amen.

*Keep alert and never give up;*
*pray always.* Ephesians 6:18

# *Rush Here, Rush There*

"Hurry up, Gail," her mother warned. "We have to be moving along."

Gail was eating breakfast. She stopped looking at the back of the cereal box and started eating faster.

"Gail, are you coming?" her mother called. "We need to leave now."

Gail was getting dressed. She stopped playing with her toys and finished putting on her shoes.

"Come on, Gail," her mother said. "You can't spend all day here."

Gail had stopped to look at something in the store window.

(Did you ever have a day like Gail's? Someone makes you rush here, rush there. It seems that, on some days, you have to hurry up everywhere.)

"Now we don't have to hurry," Gail's mother said. It was finally nighttime. Now she and her mother had a chance to be together, to pray together. Today, especially, Gail liked this time. There was nothing to hurry for, now. Finally!

# *Dear Jesus,*

Sometimes I get too busy. Thanks for always being around to listen when I need to talk. Amen.

*Trust in the Lord and you
will be happy.* Proverbs 16:20

# See What I Can Do!

Here's a game for a spring day. Fill in each blank space. Do what each sentence says.

- I can jump as high as an _____
- I can reach as tall as the _____
- I can hop as far as _____
- I can take steps as big as _____
- I can laugh as much as _____
- I can wink like _____
- I can wiggle as fast as _____
- I can smile because _____

# Dear Jesus,

Prayer suggestion: Jesus gives us lots of reasons to be happy. Tell Him what has made you happy today.

*You made summer and winter.*
Psalm 74:16–17.

# "*It's Not Warm Enough!*"

What a beautiful day! The sun was shining. A warm breeeze was blowing. Erica thought it was a perfect day to play in water.

"Mommy, can I put on my swimsuit and run through the hose?" Erica asked.

"No, Erica, it's not warm enough," her mother answered.

"Well, then, can I fill up the swimming pool?"

"No, Erica, it's not warm enough," her mother said.

"Can I get out the squirt guns and spray water on me?" Erica asked. (What do you think her mother said?)

"It's not fun today," Erica said. "You never let me do anything I want."

"Erica, you know that's not true," her mother said. "Let's take down the thermometer and work with that. It will be fun."

They unclipped the thermometer from outside the kitchen window. Erica's mother put different pieces of tape at different temperatures. On one piece of tape toward the bottom Mother wrote, "Wear a hat and coat." Another piece of tape, higher up, said, "Wear a jacket." Erica's favorite piece of tape said, "Barefoot, swimsuit."

When will it be warm enough for you to play outside in water? Ask an adult to help you make a thermometer the way Erica and her mother did.

# *Dear Jesus,*

Sometimes I try to make spring days warmer than they really are. Thanks for all different kinds of weather. When it gets hot, I know I will like to _____ . Amen.

*The world and all that is in it*
*belong to the Lord.* Psalm 24:1

# Keep God's World Beautiful

The sky was getting dark. Thunder began to roll. A few drops started to fall. Sheila and Ramona raced inside. "Girls, you look afraid," Sheila's mother said. "What's wrong?"

"It's starting to rain," Ramona said fearfully. "We just talked about dirty rain at school."

"It's terrible, Mommy," Sheila added. "Smoke from chimneys and big trucks goes up to the sky and makes the clouds dirty. Then we get yucky rain."

"God never should've made rain," Ramona said. "That polluted rain can hurt us and fish and my flowers and . . . "

"Wait a minute, Ramona," Sheila's mother said. "It's not God's fault we have dirty rain. We just haven't been careful with the nice world God made for us."

Ramona and Sheila were quiet for a minute. They remembered the Bible story about when God created the world. It must have been beautiful.

"You can help make the world a better place, girls," Sheila's mother said gently. "Can you think how?"

Ramona looked outside the window. There was the popsicle paper left on the grass. She would clean that up when the rain stopped.

Sheila thought of something she could do, too. What could Sheila do to help keep God's world beautiful?

# Dear Jesus,

Help me remember to keep Your world a nice place to live. Amen.

*God loved the world so much*
*that He gave His only Son.*
John 3:16

# What Comes First?

Let's play a game. Think of what comes first in these actions, then fill in the blanks:

- You need a Kleenex before you blow your _____ .
- You need to put on your socks before you put on your _____ .
- You put the cereal in the bowl before you _____ .
- Jesus died on a cross before I could go to _____ .
- (This last sentence is really important.) If it hadn't been for Jesus, we never could have _____ .

# Dear Jesus,

Prayer suggestion: Thank Jesus for loving you so that you could love Him back.

*Remember your Creator*
*while you are still young.*
Ecclesiastes 12:1a

# The Original Helmet

It was so warm today, Elizabeth could hardly believe it was still spring. As she rode in the car with her dad, the air rushed through the open window and cooled her sweaty hair.

"Those workers must really be hot," she said. Her dad was driving past a construction site. Many people were working hard; most wore hard hats.

"Their heads must really be sweating," Elizabeth said.

A sudden noise outside the car window brought a zooming motorcycle next to the car.

"That driver's wearing a helmet, too," Elizabeth said excitedly.

"Lots of people wear protective head coverings," her dad said. (Who else can you think of?)

"Of course," Dad added, "God made us the best helmet of all."

"I don't understand, Dad," Elizabeth said.

"God made our skulls to cover the soft brain parts in our head," her dad said. "That was a great idea."

"God does have lots of good ideas," said Elizabeth.

# Dear Jesus,

Thanks for all the wonderful things You do. I know the best thing You did for me was to have Jesus die so that my sins would be forgiven. Amen.

*Give thanks to the greatest of
all gods; His love is eternal.*
Psalm 136:1–3

# A Present That's Not Wrapped

April was very excited. One of her favorite people, Nana, was coming to visit. Nana hadn't sent April a birthday present this year, but maybe Nana would just bring it along today.

There she was!

"Nana, Nana," April threw her arms around Nana. "I'm so glad you're here."

"How big you are!" Nana said. "You're not my little baby any more. You're a big girl."

"What did you get me, Nana?" April asked. "What did you buy me for my birthday?"

Nana's smile faded.

"Oh, April; I forgot your present," Nana said. "I'm so sorry!" April was so disappointed, she almost started to cry.

Nana knelt down beside April. She put her arm around her. "I'm very sorry that I don't have a present all wrapped up for you," Nana explained. "But while I'm visiting, I'll try to give you a different kind of gift. I'll spend lots of time with you. We'll go on some walks together. And I'll read a bunch of stories to you."

April looked up. "Good, Nana," April said. "A present doesn't have to be in a box."

## Dear Jesus,

Thank You for Your special gift of love. Amen.

*The righteous will flourish*
*like palm trees.* Psalm 92:12–14.

# Seein' Green

Look out your window. During late spring many growing things turn a beautiful green color. Find eight things that are green.

Now look inside your house. Can you find eight things inside that are green?

Sometimes people don't think about the color green, but they can't forget it at this beautiful time of year. This lovely color is one of the things of life God has given us to enjoy.

Spring—what a great time to enjoy the color green! What a great time also to enjoy the life God gives each of us.

# Dear Jesus,

Thank You for the spring gift of new life outside. Thanks, too, for letting me live in Your colorful world. Amen.

*There are many rooms
in My Father's house.*
John 14:2

# Balloons in Heaven?

"Hang onto that balloon, Madeline," her mother cautioned. "A helium balloon will fly away if you let it go."

"Mommy, if I let the balloon go, would it go all the way to heaven?" Madeline asked.

"It would go far into the sky," her mother said.

"But would it go to Grandpa in heaven?" Madeline asked again.

"I'm sure Grandpa is very happy being with Jesus," her mother said. "He probably doesn't need a green balloon."

"Will they have a birthday cake for Grandpa?" Madeline asked. "Will they know that his favorites are chocolate cake and chocolate frosting?"

"Oh, Madeline," her mother said. "Grandpa doesn't need a birthday cake in heaven."

"Well, I think he wants a green balloon," said Madeline. "I always liked sharing with Grandpa."

Madeline let go of her balloon. She and her mother watched the green balloon sail up to the sky.

That night Madeline and her mother talked more about heaven. Her mother read in the Bible about heaven. You can read about it, too. Just look in John 14:1–4.

# Dear Jesus,

Thank You for the place in heaven that is waiting for me. Amen.

*Who is it that feeds the ravens*
*when they wander about hungry?*
Job 38:39–39:1

# *Thanks, God, for Goldfish*

[This is a good story to act out. Read the devotion aloud first. Then encourage your child to "be Faye" as you read it aloud again.]

Faye was so excited! They were going to pick up her new dog. She had been counting the days, and this was it. The puppy was now old enough to leave its mother.

Faye cuddled her dog all the way home in the car. It was so soft, so little! That night, though, Faye had a runny nose.

The next day Faye played with her new puppy whenever it wasn't sound asleep. That night, though, Faye's eyes started to get red. Her nose was still very sniffly.

During the next few days Faye loved her puppy more and more. And her sniffles got worse and worse. The doctor said she was allergic to her new dog. They would have to give it away.

Faye cried and cried. Even when they found a friend who would love and care for the puppy, Faye was unhappy. Faye's daddy said she could get another pet, but Faye wasn't sure she could love a different pet.

It was a horrible week at Faye's house. Then, on Friday night, this was Faye's bedtime prayer: "Thanks, God, for goldfish."

Faye felt better now that she would have a pet that didn't cause allergy problems.

What kind of pet do you think Faye got?

# *Dear Jesus,*

Thank You for so many different animals. For animals I see outside the window, like _____ . For animals I see at the zoo, like _____ .And for animals I can play with, like _____ .
Amen.

*Christ has been raised
from death.* 1 Corinthians 15:20

# *All Gone*

Colette and Leo had loved watching the grass grow longer and greener. It was exciting to see how plants grew bigger. (What have you liked about this spring?)

One thing made Colette and Leo sad, though. The bird's nest they had watched with excitement was now empty. The little birds had grown up and gone away. When Leo looked at the empty nest, he felt empty inside, too.

"Being empty is sometimes good," their mother said. "Remember when you couldn't wait to have the first empty space in your mouth, Leo?"

"When I lost my tooth!" Leo remembered.

"And you know how exciting it is to empty your toy box," their mother reminded them. "Empty isn't always bad."

"And in Sunday school we sing happy songs about the empty tomb on Easter," Colette said. "Empty was good on Easter."

"And an empty nest is a good sign, too," their mother said. "Those two little birds have grown up enough to take care of themselves."

Will you have fun dumping out buckets of sand at a beach this summer? Has your shoe ever felt better after you emptied out some rocks? Think of times when "empty" has been good.

An empty tomb at Easter was a great thing for us all. That meant Jesus had risen. Hallelujah!

# *Dear Jesus,*

Prayer suggestion: Say a thank-You prayer to Jesus.

*He showed me Jerusalem.*
Revelation 21:10–21

# Magic Carpets

"Rain, rain, go away . . . " the children said. It had rained for three days. They couldn't play outside. They were bored.

"What can we do?" Mari Jean asked her dad. "There's nothing at all to do."

Her dad thought for a moment. "We will go to far-off lands," he said with a smile. "We will take a magic carpet ride!"

Mari Jean and her brother helped her dad put the sofa cushions on the living room floor. They scattered chair cushions in different places, too.

The children ran to their bedrooms and packed for the trip. This was going to be fun!

Everybody found a "magic carpet." They sat on their pillow and told where they were going. Then, when the timer rang five minutes later, they climbed onto another magic carpet and went to a different place.

"I'm going to an island this time," Mari Jean announced. "It's a good thing I brought my crayons."

"I'm going to look for penguins," said her brother. He was looking at his book about polar bears and birds of the arctic.

"I'm going up to heaven," their dad said. "I just want to look around. Have a great trip, you two."

If you could go on a magic carpet to heaven, whom would you visit? What would you see? You can read about heaven in Revelation 21:10–21.

# Dear Jesus,

Prayer suggestion: Talk to Jesus about heaven.

---

*Leave all your worries
with Him.* 1 Peter 5:6–7

# Worried?

Everybody was having fun, splashing in the water. Splash! Whoosh! Everybody was having fun. Everybody except Lucy. She just sat on the side of the backyard. Her swimsuit wasn't even wet.

"What's wrong with Lucy?" Kelly asked.

"Just leave her alone," somebody answered.

"She's so crabby she's not fun, anyway," another one said.

Lucy still just sat there.

"What's wrong?" Kelly asked.

"Nothing," said Lucy.

"Something must be wrong," Kelly said. "You're never like this, all sad and frowny."

"My mom's in the hospital," Lucy explained. "I saw her yesterday, and she didn't look like she used to."

"What was she doing?" Kelly asked.

"She was just lying in a bed," Lucy said. "When she's home, she's always running around the house. I never saw her just lying on a bed at lunchtime. It was scary."

Have you ever visited a hospital? Talk to someone about what you saw. When you know about a hospital, it won't seem so scary.

# Dear Jesus,

Thank You for doctors and nurses and all the other people who work at hospitals to help people feel better. Amen.

*Pray at all times.*
1 Thessalonians 5:16–18.

# *"I'm So Tired!"*

It had been a long day for Sara. She couldn't wait to crawl into bed. Off came the shoes; next the clothes. Then the pajamas went on.

"I'm too tired to brush my teeth," Sara complained.

"Okay," said her dad. "Just this once."

"I'm too tired to pick up the things in my room," Sara said.

"Okay; you can do it in the morning," her dad said.

"I'm too tired to pray," said Sara.

"No, Sara; that's not something we skip," her dad said. "God gave us this wonderfully busy day. We can at least say 'thank You.' "

This was Sara's prayer:

"Dear Jesus, when You were little, I think You got tired just like I am. Thank You for this wonderful day. Amen."

And Sara fell right to sleep.

# *Dear Jesus,*

Prayer suggestion: Have you ever had such a busy day that you wanted to skip talking to Jesus? Jesus will listen to a short prayer or a long prayer. He just likes to listen to what you say. Pray to Him now.

*Always give thanks for*
*everything to God.* Ephesians 5:20

# Snack on a Stick

[As you read this, ask your child to make a growling sound each time you read, "Peter's stomach rumbled."]

"Hey, Dad," Peter said. "We're all hungry." *Peter's stomach rumbled.*

"It's not time for lunch, guys," his father said.

"But we're starved," Peter said. *Peter's stomach rumbled.*

"Okay," his dad said. "I'll see what I can come up with."

Pretty soon his dad came out of the house. "Find some thin sticks, guys, and peel off the bark." *Peter's stomach rumbled.*

"Dad, we can't eat sticks," Peter said. *Peter's stomach rumbled.*

"Of course not," said his dad. "But we're just starting off the summer fruit season, so here's your first stick-snack of the year. Now, watch what I do." *Peter's stomach rumbled.*

He took a melon ball from the tray and stuck it all the way to the end of a peeled stick. Then he did the same with a big strawberry and a grape. Soon he had the whole stick covered with fresh fruit. *Peter's stomach rumbled.*

"That's a summer stick-snack, guys," his dad said. "Now, let's pray together and then dig in."

"Pray?" one of Peter's friends asked. "It's not bedtime."

"We always give thanks for our food here," his dad said. "These are fruits we haven't enjoyed since last summer, and I'm sure we'll want to thank God for giving us such a wonderful snack. Here. I'll pray with you." Peter's stomach smiled. And so did Peter as his dad prayed. (What was Peter's dad's prayer?)

# Dear Jesus,

Prayer suggestion: Thank God for your favorite summer foods.

*Their father loved Joseph.*
Genesis 37:4

## *Joe and His Coat*

Fred was going to a puppet show. Actually, his mother had explained, there would be several shows. Children at church had worked on making puppets, a stage, and even had written the words their puppets would say. Fred had never been to a puppet show. This would be fun.

Fred thought the puppets were great. His favorite show was "Joe and His Coat." The story had been about a boy, Joseph, whose father gave him a coat. "Thanks, Dad," Puppet Joe said. "The colors match my sandals." Fred had laughed at Puppet Joe.

When Fred got home, he wanted to do a puppet show, too. The back of the sofa would be a great stage. But where could he find a good story for puppets?

"Try the Bible," his mother suggested.

"The Bible is just for big people," Fred said.

"Most of the stories you hear at church are from the Bible," his mother said. "That puppet show you liked best today, 'Joe and His Coat,' was from the Bible."

Fred and his mother sat down with the Bible. Fred couldn't read yet, but his mother read him the story about Joseph. You can read that story, too, in Genesis 37:1–11.

What Bible story could you make into a puppet show? Ask an adult to help you.

## *Dear Jesus,*

I know You loved Joseph of the Bible. You took care of him.
I know You love me. You will take care of me, too. Amen.

*Friends always show
their love.* Proverbs 17:17

# A Ducky Day!

Orlanda and her mother were feeding the ducks at the park. Other children and even some adults were laughing at the ducks. Orlanda smiled at someone, but then Orlanda looked puzzled. Orlando thought that the person who smiled back at her looked different.

"Mommy, what's wrong with that girl's face?" Orlanda asked quietly.

"I'm not sure," her mother answered, "but she might have Down's Syndrone."

"Is that like chicken pox without spots?" Orlanda asked.

"No," said her mother. "It's something that happened to her long before she was born. If that girl has Down's, it just means she will have a harder time learning some things. But she sure knows how to feed the ducks. Look how they follow her!"

Orlanda ran over to her new friend and smiled. Maybe Orlanda could learn how to make ducks follow her, too.

Orlanda and the other girl had a wonderful time at the park that day. Orlanda learned there was only one thing better than feeding ducks; she had lots more fun feeding ducks with a friend!

Draw a picture of you and a friend having fun.

# Dear Jesus,

Thank You for friends to talk to, play with, and learn from. Amen.

*The disciples got into the boat in
which Jesus was already sitting.*
Mark 4:35–39.

# Alone in a Crowd?

[As you read this, ask the child to pretend with you that you are in a boat. Keep rocking as you read!]

Hazel had looked forward to this boat ride for a long time. Her first time on a real boat! Mommy and Daddy were having a great time talking to their friends. Everybody on the boat seemed happy.

Everybody except Hazel. The gentle bouncing on the waves made her stomach feel dizzy.

The bright sun shone on the water, but that made Hazel's eyes hurt. She squinted and looked around. Mommy and Daddy were right there, but she felt all alone. Nobody was paying any attention to her. And besides, she wasn't having fun at all.

Hazel didn't know what to do. (What would you have done?)

Then Hazel had an idea. She would sing a song from church—just to herself, of course. That might help. Her teacher had said that Jesus is always with us. Maybe if she sang a song she wouldn't feel so lonesome.

Hazel sang very quietly, just to herself. She started to feel better. Then she whispered another song. This boat ride was getting to be fun.

Hazel's mother looked over at her and smiled.

What do you think she told Hazel?

# Dear Jesus,

Thank You for always being with me. Sometimes I forget that I always have You as a friend. Amen.

*You make . . . plants for man to use.* Psalm 104:14–15

# Underground Food

Paulo tugged and tugged. The dandelion just wouldn't come up.

"Be sure you get the root," his mother cautioned. "Otherwise, that weed will be growing right back again."

"Why did God make plants have roots, anyway?" Paulo asked. "It just is so hard to weed."

"It's a good thing God made roots for plants," Paulo's mother answered. "You wouldn't have your favorite sweet potato pie without a root. You know, a sweet potato is an underground food."

Miranda, Paulo's older sister, added, "And what about the radishes and carrots we'll be pulling up to eat in a few weeks? You love those foods."

As Paulo pulled out the whole dandelion root, he said with a smile, "Finally! That's one big dandelion gone forever." He threw it into the weed bag.

"Paulo," his mother said, "just remember that God always takes care of us, even when our food hides under the ground."

# Dear Jesus,

Thank You for food that grows on trees, like _____ .

Thank You for food that grows on top of the ground, like _____ .

Thank You for food that grows under the ground, like _____ .
Amen.

*We will always praise You.*
Psalm 44:8

# Time for Bed

"Ricky, time for bed," his father called. "Brush your teeth."

"Dad, it can't be bedtime already," Ricky said. "Everybody else is staying up."

"Ricky, it is bedtime for *you*," his dad explained. "Each of you kids has a different bedtime. You each need different amounts of sleep."

"Well, it's just not fair," Ricky complained.

"We'll talk about it when I come to pray with you," his dad said. "But now, brush your teeth."

When Ricky's dad came into the bedroom for prayers, Ricky still had a frown on his face. It was no fun being the youngest, especially at bedtime.

"If I was born first, I could stay up last," Ricky pouted.

"That's true," his dad said. "If you were the oldest, you could also cut the grass and help with the shopping." Ricky thought about that. Maybe being littlest in the family wasn't so bad.

"Dad, when I get older, will you still tuck me in at night?" Ricky asked. "Will you still pray with me?"

"I'll do that as long as you'd like," his dad answered. "Now, let's pray."

# Dear Jesus,

Prayer suggestion: Say a prayer with Ricky, thanking God for the things you did today.

*The Lord . . . [is] the Creator of*
*heaven, earth, and sea.*
Psalm 146:5–6

# 'Round and 'Round

Have you ever been to a fair or park that has things that go 'round and 'round? What are some things you can think of that move like that? Take your finger and make circles and circles. That might give you some ideas.

In the summertime, children ride on many kinds of things that go around.

What's something that goes around and is high in the air, then low on the ground? What's something that goes around and around very fast? Did you think of things like merry-go-rounds and little racing cars? Those can be great fun.

You're going around right now. You might not feel it, but the earth is turning. Our earth is always going around. God made it that way.

As you get older, you will learn more about how our earth moves. You will learn about other things in our universe that move, too. God has made a wonderful place for us to live. He's created interesting things for us to explore and learn about.

As you study about comets and planets and satellites, remember that God created everything. He is a wonderful and powerful God. "Creator of the Universe" is one way to describe God. And do you know what? That's exactly right.

# *Dear God,*

Prayer suggestion: Say a prayer to God as Creator of the universe.

---

*His Son . . . Savior.* John 3:17

# Alike and Different

Play this game with the person who's reading this book to you. As each of you answers the questions, talk about ways you are the same, and ways you are different.

- What color is your hair?
- What is your favorite summer food?
- What do you like to do at the beach?
- What is your favorite day in the summer months?
- Who loves you?

There are lots of ways to answer that last question. But there's one answer you and everybody can give: God loves you. He loves everyone.

We are all different in some ways. But we are all alike in one way: God loves us. And that's good news for today and every day.

# Dear Jesus,

Prayer suggestion: Spend a minute now to talk with God.

*You know the way.* John 14:4–6

# *Map Fun*

[To help your child better understand this devotion, make a "relief map" together in the sandbox. Build mountains, tunnel out some rivers and highways, even add cardboard buildings.]

Andy stood quietly behind his father. His dad had been studying the maps for a long time now.

"What's a map for?" Andy finally asked.

"A map shows all different places and how to get there," his dad answered. "I'm figuring out the roads we'll take on our vacation."

"What are all those blue places?" Andy wanted to know. (Could you tell Andy? Look at a real map if possible.)

"Blue is for water," Andy's dad answered.

"What about those red lines?" Andy asked next.

"Those are the big highways," his dad said. "I think we'll be going on one of them for a long way."

"How do we get to Grandma's?" Andy asked. His dad showed him the way.

"How do we get to Uncle Wallace's?" Dad showed him the way.

"How do we get to Disney World?" His dad showed him the way.

"How to we get to heaven?" Andy asked finally.

"That's not on this map," said Andy's dad. "The Bible is our map for heaven."

"I never saw little red lines and blue lakes in the Bible," Andy said.

"Oh, Andy," his dad laughed. "Jesus tells us that we need to believe in Him as our Savior. Then we don't need a map."

# *Dear Jesus,*

I like many places. I always have fun when I go to _____ . I laugh when I go to _____ . Thank You for having a place for me in heaven. Amen.

*You will be witnesses*
*for me.* Acts 1:8

# Grown-up Jobs

Patty rubbed her hand carefully over the bandage on her arm. It still hurt where she had gotten the shot.

"I'm sure not going to be a doctor when I grow up," Patty told her mother. "Nobody would like you, because you give shots."

"Sometimes a person has to hurt in order to help someone else," her mother said. "That sounds strange, but that shot will keep you from getting a terrible illness."

"I still think being a doctor is an icky job—except if you help people have babies," Patty said.

"There are good parts and not-so-good parts about any work," her mother said. "I love my job, but I don't like being away from you so much of the time."

"I'm going to find a job that is fun and, when you have it, everybody likes you," Patty said. She was quiet for a while, just thinking.

"I know!" Patty said. "I'll tell people about Jesus. That's a big job, and everybody wants to hear more about Jesus."

Patty is thinking about when she grows up. But she could tell people about Jesus right now, even though she is still young. So can you. Which of your friends can you talk to about Jesus? Whom can you invite to church with you?

# Dear Jesus,

Prayer suggestion: Talk to God now about how you can tell others about Jesus.

*There will always be cold and heat,*
*summer and winter, day and night.*
Genesis 8:22.

# *Why Does the Sun Shine?*

"Why does God make the sun shine?" Roger asked.

"So our vegetables will grow in the garden," said his mom.

"Why else?" asked Roger.

"So I can cut the grass with the new mower," said his mother.

"Why else?" asked Roger.

"So it looks like a perfect summer day," said his mother.

"But why else does God make the sun shine?" Roger asked.

"I just don't know," said his mother.

"So I can wear my new swimsuit and lie in the sun on my new beach towel," said Roger. "That's why God makes the sun shine!"

"That's a very good reason," said his mother.

Did the sun shine at your house today? How would you describe the weather where you live?

# *Dear God,*

Thank You for all sorts of days. For the gentle rain that helps the flowers grow. For the wind that blows the seeds around to start new plants. And for the bright, sunny summer days. Thanks, God, for always smiling at me. Amen.

*Help carry one another's
burdens.* Galatians 6:2

# A Good Kind of Tired

"Daddy, why are you so tired after work?" Chona asked.

"I have a 'feeling job,' Chona," her father answered. "That makes me very tired."

"What does that mean, Daddy?" Chona asked. "Do you touch people who come to your office?"

"Oh, no, Chona," her father laughed. He explained that a counselor tries to help people with their problems. People can come and talk to him about things they need help with; then he listens. He feels their problems almost as though they were his own. Sometimes he can help.

"Ana's mother is tired after work, too," Chona said. "She helps people, too."

Chona was quiet for a moment. She was thinking of some other helping people.

(Whom can you think of?)

"It's a good kind of tired, though," Chona's father said. "I feel happy inside that I can help people."

"Pastor Martin must feel a good kind of tired, too," said Chona. "He helps people all the time."

Chona was right about her pastor. Does your minister feel a good kind of tired from helping people? Does he like telling people about Jesus?

Ask your pastor about his job. Maybe you will have a "feeling job" when you grow up.

# Dear Jesus,

Thank You for these people who tell me about Jesus: _____
_____. Amen.

*God sent the Spirit of His Son*
*into our hearts.* Galatians 4:4–7

# Half and Half

"I just got a new dog," said Rudi. "He's half beagle and half something else."

"My dog is part Pointer and part Lab," said Suvi.

Flossie was quiet. She didn't have a dog. She didn't have a cat or any pet.

Then she had a great idea. "I'm part my mom's and part Jesus' child," she said. "Half and half make a whole—so that's me!"

Flossie was trying to explain whose child she was. How would you explain whose child you are?

# Dear Jesus,

I like being Your child. Amen.

*Let us go to*
*the Lord's house.* Psalm 122:1

# A Special Friend

[Ask your child to stand up while you read this devotion. Encourage your child to act out the action words that are italicized. Have fun!]

Today was a special day for Anna. Her friend Evelyn had invited her to watch *baton twirling* practice.

Anna felt so grown up. Evelyn was a teenager. She helped teach Anna's class at Sunday school. Anna liked Evelyn so much. Sometimes Evelyn baby-sat for Anna.

Now Anna could watch Evelyn practice for *marching in a parade.*

Evelyn started practicing by *lying on the ground.* Anna thought that was funny, but Evelyn said that baton twirlers first must *stretch* their bodies. Then she *jogged!*

When Evelyn finished warming up, she took the baton and tried some *twirls, circles* and *spins* from the routine she would do during the parade. Anna thought Evelyn was beautiful, even without a pretty costume.

"Evelyn, when I grow up, I want to be just like you," Anna said. "I want to go to the same school, take *twirling* lessons, and everything!"

Evelyn said. "You'll be your very own person, Anna. I'm glad you want to be like me, but you'll be you. And that's nice, too."

Anna was quiet for a minute. Then she had an idea. "Well, at least we can still *go to* the same *church* together!" (What friends do you see at church?)

# Dear Jesus,

Thank You for letting me go to a church where I can see my friends and learn about You. Amen.

*I will be with you always.*
Matthew 28:20b

# Moving Around

Moving your body can be fun. Can you move an ankle? Now move your heel. Now move your elbow. Moving *can* be fun!

But when you move your body from your house in your town to another house in another town and never move back, that's hard. A moving van can carry your toys, books, even the refrigerator. But your friends can't go with you. You can't move a favorite tree or even the view you see from your bedroom. That's when moving is hard.

But Jesus always is with you. He's with you when you move your body for fun—when you move your hands or feet or tummy. He's with you when it's hard to move from one place to another to live. You never have to pack Jesus. He'll move right along with you.

# Dear Jesus,

Thank You for always being with me. When I move from place to place or when I just move me, I know You're there. Amen.

*The Lord will protect you.*
Psalm 121:7–8

# My Home

Today we're playing a game. See if you can answer these riddles:

- Goldfish swim in a _____ . [bowl]
- A gopher digs a deep _____ . [hole]
- A bat flies into a _____ . [cave]
- A whale swims over a _____ . [wave]
- A snail carries his _____ . [house]
- A trap is not a good place for a _____ . [mouse]
- A pig lives in a _____ . [pen]
- A bear lives in a _____ . [den]
- A bird lives in a _____ . [nest]
- But where I live is the _____ ! [best]

# Dear Jesus,

Thank You for giving me a place to live. Sometimes I forget to thank You for that. My favorite thing about where I live is _____ _____ . Amen.

*God . . . loved us.* 1 John 4:10–11

# A Good Game?

Did you ever do this with your friends? Listen as Nancy and Rudy talk.

Nancy: "I can zipper."

Rudy: "Well, I can tie."

Nancy: "I could button when I was two years old."

Rudy: "When I was born I could do that."

Rudy and Nancy are playing a game that isn't much fun. Adults call it "one-upmanship." People try to say things that will make them feel they are better than another person. Nobody wins at that game, and everybody starts to feel bad.

Some people foolishly think, "Jesus loves me better than you." *That's not true.* Jesus loves everyone just the same, and *more* than they know. Jesus died on the cross for everybody.

The special thing about Jesus is that He's not playing a game. Jesus is for real. And that can make us all feel so good!

# Dear Jesus,

It's not easy always being nice. Help me to show the kind of love that You showed when You died for me. Amen.

*Every year the parents of Jesus
went to Jerusalem.* Luke 2:41

# It's Always Hot

"My, you have hot summers here," Grandma said to Zabelle.

"We have hot everything," Zabelle said. "It's sweating hot in summer. Even at Christmas it's sort of warm. We only wear a sweater on Christmas."

"We sure could use some of your warm weather up where I live," Grandma said. "It's so cold that sometimes I don't even want to take out the garbage."

(Where do you think Zabelle's grandma lived? Do different seasons cause weather changes where you live?)

"I wish I lived where you live, Grandma," Zabelle said. "It's always the same here."

"Well, Zabelle, let me tell you—God made a wonderful place when He created earth," Grandma said. "Some places stay pretty much the same all year. That's how it was where Jesus lived."

"Really, Grandma?" Zabelle asked. "You mean, Jesus always had hot feet, too?"

"Well, I can't say for sure," Grandma said. "It probably got a mite cold at night in the mountains. But most days the little boy Jesus probably had weather pretty much like the little girl Zabelle."

Zabelle was quiet. It was exciting to think that Jesus was her age once. She wondered if He had friends. She wondered about the kind of school Jesus went to.

If you want to read about Jesus when He was a little boy, look at the story in Luke 2:41–52. You will learn about a family trip Jesus took when He was about 12 years old.

# Dear Jesus,

It's good to remember that You started out as a child, just like me. You know what it's like to be _____years old. Amen.

*Being wise is better
than being strong.* Proverbs 24:5

# Keeping Cool

"Oooh," Lynn said. "Look at that pig!"

A great big pig was almost swimming in mud. It plopped on one side and then turned over to cover the rest of its body in mud.

"Yuck," said Lynn, "I'm glad I'm not a pig. Mrs. Harris, why do they like to get so dirty?" Mrs. Harris was a farmer.

"I'm not sure pigs like to get dirty," Mrs. Harris said. "But wallowing in mud helps the pigs stay cool on hot days like this.

"Pigs don't sweat, they don't perspire as we do to keep cool on days like this," the farmer continued. "Also, mud won't let them get sunburned."

Lynn laughed. She couldn't imagine a sunburned pig.

"Mud also protects pigs from getting bitten by lots of insects," Mrs. Harris added.

"I never knew pigs were so smart," Lynn said. "That's a really good idea."

"Actually, God takes care of pigs just as He cares for everything else on this farm," Mrs. Harris said.

"He takes better care of me," Lynn said. "I don't have to roll in mud to keep cool!"

# Dear Jesus,

I know You taught birds how to make nests and pigs how to keep cool. Thank You for letting people a long time ago write the Bible so that I know about You. That's most important of all. Amen.

*You made summer.* Psalm 74:16–17

## *Summer Sillies*

[Encourage your child to pretend during this devotion. Have your child act out the italicized actions of Billie Jo's mother.]

Billie Jo was sweating. It was terribly hot. She hated summer.

"I'm tired of this weather," she complained to her mother. "There's nothing to do but get hot."

"Oh, Billie Jo," said her mother. "It's time to play a game. Let's think of all the things we can do just in summer."

Billie Jo watched in amazement as her mother stood up and started *marching around* the kitchen.

"What are you doing?" Billie Jo asked.

"I'm marching in a parade," her mother said. "Remember what fun you had the other day *carrying a flag?* You couldn't do that in winter."

Her mother sat down and *licked the air*. What do you think her mother was acting out now?

"You're eating an ice cream bar," Billie Jo said. "I don't believe it, though, Mommy. You never act silly like this."

"That's one of the fun things about summer," her mother smiled. "Summer sillies are great fun for everybody."

Billie Jo smiled. Maybe summer wasn't so bad!

What can you act out that you do only in summer? Ask the person reading this book to act out something, too. And have fun. It's summer, one of God's great times of the year.

## *Dear Jesus,*

Thank You for the summertime, a time when I can do all kinds of things, like _____

_____ . Amen.

*Isn't He the carpenter's son?*
Matthew 13:55

# A Good Helper

Curt knew today would be beastly hot. Breakfast was barely over, and already the sun was burning. There wasn't a cloud in the sky. What a day to have to work outside with his dad!

Curt and his dad collected the tools they needed. They would be weeding the garden, trimming bushes, and cleaning out the flower beds. (What kinds of tools did they take outside?)

Curt liked to be with his dad. He just wished the weather wasn't so hot.

Sweat dripped down Curt's face. His hands were filthy from working in the mud. Every time he tried to clean his face, it got dirtier.

Then Curt and his dad went inside to get some cool water. His dad smiled.

"Son, this is tough work," Dad said. "But you're a great help. I'm sure Joseph was just as glad to have help in the carpentry shop a long time ago."

Curtis smiled. It felt good that Dad needed him. He'd work even harder than ever, now. But Joseph? They didn't know a Joseph who was a carpenter.

Then Curt smiled again. He remembered whom his dad was talking about. Do you know?

# Dear Jesus,

Thank You for the chance to be with people who help us work. Amen.

*Pray at all times.*
1 Thessalonians 5:16–18

# No Lights!

The thunder crashed and the lightning crackled. Suddenly the TV blinked off. The lights in the living room went off, too. Mickey tried the kitchen lights. Nothing happened. Dad tried to call the electric company. The phone didn't work.

"The storm knocked down wires somewhere," Mickey's dad said.

"What can we do?" Mickey asked.

"We'll wait until things get fixed," his dad said. "Meanwhile, let's see what still works."

"We can play my radio," Mickey said. "It has batteries."

"The cuckoo clock still works," Mickey's uncle said. "I know it's near supper, so I'll fix some sandwiches."

Soon the family gathered around the supper table. The lights still hadn't come on. The phone still didn't work.

"At least we can pray," Mickey said. "Jesus still works!"

Walk around your house and see what is electrically powered. What would still work if the electricity went off?

# Dear Jesus,

I know You are always with me. When I'm scared or afraid, I can always talk to You. I can tell You about things that make me happy, too. Thank You, Jesus, for being You. Amen.

*God's message is near you,*
*on your lips and in your heart.*
Romans 10:8

## "*Pack Up—Let's Go!*"

Vacation time was getting closer and closer. Every day Vivian marked off another day on the calendar. Finally, packing day arrived.

"Let's think from head to toe," her daddy said. "That way we won't miss anything you'll need."

Help Vivian pack.

For her head she'll pack _____

For her body she'll pack _____

For her feet she'll pack _____

Vivian will be going swimming a lot. Pack her beach bag, too.

For her head she'll pack _____

For her body she'll pack _____

For her feet she'll pack _____

(Did you remember the suntan lotion?)

Vivian and her dad closed the suitcase. Then they pulled shut the beach bag.

"But, Daddy, we forgot something," Vivian said, "the book we use to talk to Jesus every night. And I don't know where to pack it. It's not part of my head or my body or my feet."

"We'll take that book in the car with the maps," her daddy said. "That way we'll be sure to remember to take our *Little Visits with Jesus* along. But Jesus Himself lives in your heart."

## *Dear Jesus,*

Prayer suggestion: Jesus lives in your heart, too. How does that make you feel? Tell Jesus in a prayer.

*We did it to be an example*
*for you to follow.*
2 Thessalonians 3:8–9

# A Thank-You Day

Sandy snuggled deeper under the covers. Outside the bedroom she could hear the storm. Thunder crashed. Lightning flashed. Even though it was the middle of the night, the lightning made the sky seem bright.

Then Sandy remembered—she had left her brand-new, red fire truck outside. It was on the porch, but it would certainly get wet.

Quickly she got out of bed and turned on the bedroom light. She reached for her bathrobe—and saw her truck sitting on her dresser. Someone had brought it in for her. What a relief! Sandy turned the light off and ran back into bed.

The next day Sandy was extra nice to everybody at her house. She didn't know who had saved her truck from the storm, so she would help everyone as a thank-you. She helped her mom tie up the tomato plants. She helped her brother sweep a corner of the garage. Sandy even helped take out the smelly-smelly garbage.

That night at bedtime Sandy remembered the nice day. She had worked hard, but she felt good about being helpful. This was her prayer:

"Dear Jesus, I feel happy as I talk to You tonight. I feel so good inside me. I wonder if that's how You felt when You died on the cross. I know it couldn't have been nice, but I think You felt good inside. Well, it's time to go to sleep. Talk to You tomorrow, Jesus."

How do you feel after hearing Sandy's prayer?

# Dear Jesus,

Prayer suggestion: Ask Jesus to help you make tomorrow a thank-you day for people you love.

*Who can tell all the great things*
*He has done?* Psalm 106:1–2

# *A Muddy-Muddy-Muddy*

Robin and Quina were having a great time. First they mixed up some mud. The mud was cool, wet, and, oh, so muddy. Then they put it in a leftover egg carton. Then they let the mud dry. Soon they would have mud cakes!

Later that day they checked on their baking. Yes, the mud cakes were almost done. Carefully they turned over the egg carton and—plop. Out fell the mud cakes.

The girls were just setting up a pretend party when Quina's mother came out. (What do you think she said?)

"What are you two doing?" she asked.

"We're having a mud-cake party," Quina said happily.

"How in the world did you get so messy?" Quina's mother said.

"When God made mud, He made it messy," Robin replied.

What do you think Quina's mother said then?

# *Dear Jesus,*

Thanks for all the things in this world I can have fun with. When I look under a rock, I might find _____ . When I climb a tree, I might see _____ . And when I play in mud, _____ . Amen.

*Your word is a lamp
to guide me.* Psalm 119:105

## "When Will I Read?"

"Mommy, when will I read?"

Have you ever asked that question? Pretend to take a book off a shelf. Now open it up. Now pretend you are reading.

Even if you can't read words, all the things you just acted out are part of learning to read. You know how to hold a book and open it up. You know that you start at the beginning of a book. You know that a book goes from the front to the back. All those things are part of getting ready to read.

Next time you go outside, look for a stop sign. I'll bet you already know what color it is, and that it says, "Stop." You *are* learning how to read.

It won't be long before you read your own name or pick out words you know in a book.

Before long, you'll be reading really big books—all by yourself. Even the Bible. But for now, ask someone to read your favorite Bible story to you.

## Dear Jesus,

Thank You for all the good stories in the Bible. I really like the story of _____ . Amen.

*I will proclaim Your greatness,*
*my God and King. Psalm 145:1–3*

# A Sit-Down Summer

[While you read this, sit down with one leg propped up on something. Then you'll be just like Ike in this story.]

Ike felt terrible. It was only the middle of the summer, and he had a broken leg. No more swimming; no more riding up and down the driveway. And for at least a week he'd have to have his leg propped up. What could he do for a whole week sitting down? (What are some things you might do if you were Ike?)

At first Ike only looked out the window. That wasn't fun.

Next he watched television. That got very boring.

Then his mother had an idea. "Ike, if you think only about yourself all the time, the days will seem to go very slowly. Instead, why don't you do things for people? I'll call Mrs. White. Maybe you can go over there. She loves to have you sit and tell her about what it's like to be your age."

"Okay," said Ike, not very happy.

"And tomorrow you can help us work for the church bazaar," his mother said. "You can help sort yarn and count squares.

"And the next day will be even busier," his mother continued. "That's when I visit people at the nursing home. Do you think you can paint or draw pictures to take to everybody? Maybe you can use a wheelchair to deliver your pictures yourself."

"Can I use colored chalk, too?" Ike said with a little eagerness. "That makes nice summer pictures."

"Of course," said his mother. "A sit-down summer might not be as great as a walking one, but we'll make it good, anyway."

# Dear Jesus,

Prayer suggestion: How does it feel having your leg propped up? When you talk to God today, thank Him for all the things you can walk to, and for your wonderful legs.

*Whoever believes in Me will live,*
*even though he dies.* John 11:25–26.

# A Special Reminder

Cathy had spent three wonderful weeks with her grandparents and Great-Aunt Hulda. She liked being with her grandma and grandpa, but most of all Cathy enjoyed her Great-Aunt Hulda.

Great-Aunt Hulda was very old. Her hair was white; her hands had purple lines and brown spots. Great-Aunt Hulda couldn't hear very well. But Cathy and Great-Aunt Hulda became special friends.

Now it was time for Cathy to go home. The car was packed. Everyone had said good-bye—except Cathy and Great-Aunt Hulda.

(How do you think Cathy feels? How do you think Great-Aunt Hulda feels? Let's listen and see what happens.)

"I wish I could stay with you," Cathy said.

"I can't go with you," Great-Aunt Hulda said. (She couldn't always hear what Cathy said.)

"I love you," Cathy said.

"For you," Great-Aunt Hulda said. It was the lace bookmark from her Bible. She pressed it into Cathy's hand and hugged her one last time.

As Cathy rode away in the car, she waved to everyone. There were Grandma and Grandpa, and Great-Aunt Hulda sitting on the porch in her chair. As always, her Bible lay open on her lap.

Cathy held tight to the bookmark. She would always remember how special the Bible bookmark was to Great-Aunt Hulda. Now it would be very special to Cathy.

Great-Aunt Hulda died soon after summer ended. Cathy was glad *and* sad. Why do you think Cathy felt like that?

# Dear Jesus,

When I think about someone dying, I feel _____. Sometimes I feel _____. Thank You for giving me people I can talk to about dying. And help me remember that I can always talk to You. Amen.

*Your constant love reaches*
*above the heavens.* Psalm 108:4

# Playing Statues

Can you guess where Romeo is?

Romeo thought this place was his favorite on the whole vacation trip. He went from room to room in this building. Every room had lots to look at. Most rooms had paintings. Some rooms had furniture. But Romeo's favorite thing in this whole place was a statue. Actually, he liked a lot of the statues. Can you tell where Romeo was?

When Romeo got back to the motel, he played "statues." He remembered the poses of some of the statues he had seen at the art museum. Play statues with Romeo:

Be a happy statue. Now freeze . . . don't move! Now be a tired statue. Now freeze . . . don't move.

Next be a statue that has just discovered a secret. Now freeze . . . don't move.

Now be a statue of Jesus. Now *move*. Show something Jesus would do.

"Statues" is a great summer game. See if you can play it again this summer.

# Dear Jesus,

Thank You that I can feel and look many different ways. Most of all, I am thankful for You. I am also thankful for _____ . Amen.

*Lord, You have made so many things!* Psalm 104:24

# Twinkling Christmas Lights

Mattie was so excited! Visiting her cousin was great, but tonight would be the best of all. Mattie was going to look for fireflies! Mattie didn't have any fireflies where she lived.

Sure enough, when it started to get dark, Mattie looked out the window and saw little dots of light blink on and off. It was time! She got the margarine container that had been washed out. Earlier that day she had poked tiny holes in the lid.

Now Mattie and her cousin raced around the lawn. There! She caught one. Now another. This was great fun.

"Girls, time to come in now," Mattie's aunt called. "Let the lightning bugs out."

Mattie looked down at the container. Every so often one of those little fireflies would blink on a friendly "hello."

Mattie carefully opened the lid and let them fly out. How brightly they fluttered away!

Mattie had a special prayer for God that night. She said, "Thank You, God, for tonight. Now that I'm big, I think I know lots of things. But until today I didn't know about Your special fireflies. Thank You for surprising me. Amen."

Has something in God's wonderful world ever surprised you? See what you can learn about fireflies. Are they really flies? How do they light up?

If you can't find the answers, here they are: Fireflies are not really flies at all. A firefly is really a beetle. To make light, the oxygen that the firefly breathes combines with chemicals in a special "light organ" underneath the firefly.

# Dear Jesus,

Prayer suggestion: Talk to God about an animal, insect, bird, or fish that you think is special.

*How good it is to give thanks
to You, O Lord.* Psalm 92:1

# Flying High

Jan heard the noise: "Sh-sh-sh."

"Sh-sh-sh." There it was again. It seemed to come from up above.

"Sh-sh-whoosh!" What was that? Jan ran out from under the trees. Now she could see the sky.

What was making that noise?

"Sh-sh-whoosh!" Oh, there! Jan saw a beautiful, giant balloon. It was so low that Jan could see three people in the basket underneath. Jan waved.

"Sh-sh-whoosh-sh!" There went the balloon, floating over other houses, past other trees.

What a thrill! Jan watched until the balloon was just a dot in the sky.

What a special summer day!

# Dear Jesus,

Every day I thank You for food and people who love me. Every day I thank You for a place to live and a church to go to. Today I want to thank You for the special things of summer. Thank You for _____ . Amen.

---

*God loves the one who*
*gives gladly.* 2 Corinthians 9:7–8

# *$$$$$$*

"Wow! Thanks for the money, Grandpa," Robert said. He took the new quarter right to his bank. Then he opened up the hole in the bottom of the bank and shook out all his money. There was a lot. Robert carefully sorted all the money into little stacks. He turned over each coin to see who was pictured.

"Who is this?" Robert held up a quarter. His grandfather said it was a famous person.

"Well then, who is this?" Robert held up a dime. (Whose picture is on a dime?)

"Who is on a penny?" Robert asked next. (Do you know?)

Robert looked at all the famous people on his money. He was puzzled. One famous person was missing.

"Grandpa, Jesus is famous," Robert said. "Why isn't His picture on money?"

"Jesus could be on money, I guess," his grandpa answered. "But His picture would need to be on money for every country in the world.

"Our money shows famous people from our country," Grandpa said. "Jesus is important to people in all the countries of the world."

Can you draw a picture of a bill or coin with Jesus' picture on it? Could your picture be used as money anywhere on earth?

# *Dear Jesus,*

I like money. I like to count it. I like to save it. I like to spend it. Please help me remember to share it with You and with people who need it. Amen.

*I love you.* John 15:9

## Listen to Love

We hear many different sounds. Let's play a listening game:

- Make a soft sound.
- Make a squeaky sound.
- Make a sound without using your voice.

I think the sound of love is beautiful. Well . . . maybe I can't hear love, but I can hear what love does.

I heard love yesterday when a child told me, "I'm sorry."

This morning I heard a little boy comfort another boy who fell down. He said, "Let's go inside and get a Band-Aid." That was a nice sound of love.

Jesus says the words, "I love you." That's a beautiful sound.

If you are ever hurt or tired or angry, look in the Bible for Jesus' words. His "I love you" sounds so good!

Read Jesus' words in John 15:9. Then put a bookmark at that page. When you are feeling bad, you can open the Bible to those words. Even if you don't know how to read, you can know that Jesus says, "I love you."

## Dear Jesus,

Prayer suggestion: Say an "I love you" prayer to Jesus.

*The water which had come together*
*He named "Sea." Genesis 1:9–10*

# Water, Water Everywhere

What a hot day! Ellen was really sweating. She couldn't wait to get inside for a glass of water.

"I'm home, Mom," she called as she walked right to the sink. Nothing came out of the faucet.

She went to the bathroom and turned on that sink faucet. That didn't work either.

"Mom, there's no water," she called.

Her mother answered, "The plumber's here fixing a leak. The water is turned off all over the house."

What could Ellen do?

Later that day, when Ellen said her bedtime prayers, she thanked God for something very important. Ellen had never said a word of thanks for it before, but used it every day.

What did Ellen give thanks for that night?

# Dear Jesus,

Sometimes I forget to thank You for things that don't seem so important—until I don't have them. Tonight I want to thank You for water. Water tastes especially good to me when _____ . Water is lots of fun when _____ . I know I was baptized with water, too. That's most special of all. Amen.

*Ever since you were a child,*
*you have known the Holy*
*Scriptures.* 2 Timothy 3:15

# Make a "Good Book"

"It's too hot," Mimi complained.

"Yes," said her father, "it's very hot."

"I'm too hot outside," said Mimi, "I'm too hot inside. There's nothing to do."

"When I'm bored, I work in the basement," said her father. "Why don't you get out those scrap pieces of wood I gave you?"

"No," said Mimi. "It's too hot to hammer."

Mimi's mother said, "When I want something to do, I get out the sewing kit. Why don't you get out those pretty pieces of material I gave you for doll clothes?"

"No," said Mimi. "My dolls would be too hot all dressed up today."

Her grandma said, "Mimi, when I have a spare minute, I pick up my Bible and read."

"But I can't read words," said Mimi.

"Make your own 'Good Book,' " said Grandma. "Draw pictures of your favorite Bible stories. Then I'll help you put them together into a real book."

That's what Mimi worked on for the rest of the day.

What Bible stories do you think she drew? Can you make your own "Good Book"?

# Dear Jesus,

Thank You for time to do many different kinds of things. Amen.

*All living things look hopefully
to You.* Psalm 145:13b–16

# A Smelly Hike

Willie was enjoying his first nature walk. The woods were nicely cool. Everything was quiet. The group hadn't seen a snake yet—Willie was afraid he might get scared of that. Best of all, his nature bag was almost full.

Willie had found something thinner than a pencil. (What do you think he found?)

Willie had found something that would reflect the sun. (What was that?)

Willie had found something that was his favorite color: green. (What green thing did Willie put in his nature bag?)

But—oh, no! What was that awful smell?

"There was a skunk around here, folks," the leader said. "Can you smell that?"

"Yuck! It's awful!" said Willie.

"Well, Willie, that smell is the best way a skunk has to protect itself," the hike leader said. "A skunk doesn't run very fast or climb very well. It just squirts a liquid to keep enemies away."

"But it smells terrible!" Willie said.

"Yes," the leader said. "But God made each animal to have a special way to take care of itself. That liquid the skunk sprays is a pretty good protector."

God made each animal special, but He made us most special of all. In what special ways does God want us to protect and care for ourselves?

# Dear Jesus,

Thank You for making me the special person I am. Amen.

*Come to Me.* Matthew 11:28

# Fix-it Time

The fan broke yesterday at our house. The fan was helping us keep cool.

Can you pretend to be a fan? There are lots of different ways to do that. You can blow, just like a fan moves air. Try it.

You can wave your arms around. Did you move like the blades of a fan?

A fan motor makes a little noise. Can you whirr? Are you cooling the air around you?

Yesterday, at our house, we didn't know how to fix the fan. Today, though, somebody came. She was a great fan fixer. Now the air is moving around in our house and feels cooler.

Some people call Jesus a "fix-it person." They try to tell Him their problems and think He will fix everything right away.

It's good to talk to Jesus about problems. But sometimes Jesus doesn't fix problems the way *we'd* like Him to. Jesus takes care of us in the way that's best for us—whether we know it or not. He solves our problems because He loves us.

# Dear Jesus,

Prayer suggestion: Do you have a problem to share with Jesus? Tell Him about it.

*God . . . stopped working.*
Genesis 2:2–3

# Out for Breakfast

"Get up, get up," Mommy called. "We're going out for breakfast."

"Out for breakfast?" Tabitha thought. What did that mean?

Tabitha came slowly into the kitchen. Mommy was already dressed. Daddy was singing in the bathroom.

"Get dressed, Honey," Mommy said. "We're going to eat breakfast at a restaurant."

"Breakfast at a restaurant?" Tabitha asked. "Why?"

"It's the first day of vacation, and we always do fun and different things on vacation," her mother said.

Tabitha wasn't sure she wanted to get dressed up in a hurry and rush to a fancy restaurant. But she took out her clothes and started dressing. And, when Mommy came into her room, Tabitha thought, "Vacation time is going to be different this year."

"Where did vacations start?" Tabitha asked. "I mean, whose idea was it?"

"Well," her mother said slowly. "I guess it was one of God's good ideas. After He created the world, He took a break. We'll look that up in the Bible when we get home."

You can read the story of God's vacation in Genesis 2:2–3.

# Dear Jesus,

Thank You for new places to visit, new people to meet, new foods to taste, and for always being with me. Amen.

*Those who sleep in death*
*will also be raised.*
1 Corinthians 15:20–22

# Will You Die?

"I love you, Daddy,"

"Why Travis, what a nice thing to say," said Daddy. "It's not even Valentine's Day or my birthday. I like you to tell me you love me."

"If I love you enough, Daddy, maybe you won't ever die," said Travis.

"I hope you love me and love me and love me," said Daddy. "But loving me won't keep me from dying. Someday I will die, but I pray that's a long time from now."

"But I don't want you to die—ever!" said Travis.

Do you ever worry about someone dying? Talk about it now with the person who's reading to you.

# Dear Jesus,

Sometimes I wonder what would happen if I had to live without my mommy or daddy—and I get scared. When I worry about that, help me think instead about how blest I am to live with them now and with You. Thank You for love—especially Yours. Amen.

*Jesus Christ . . . is God's "Yes."*
2 Corinthians 1:19–20

# Amen, Amen

Do you know what the word "Amen" means?

"Amen" means "Yes, that's right!" Here is a clapping poem that will help you remember the meaning of "Amen." (Clap every time a star appears at a word. You'll soon discover the rhythm.)

   ★        ★  ★     ★
I know that Jesus is my God.

    ★
Amen!

   ★       ★        ★       ★
And He was born on Christmas—Yes!

    ★
That's right!

  ★  ★    ★   ★
And Jesus is the only One . . .

    ★
Amen!


   ★      ★    ★     ★
Who gave His life to save me. Yes!

    ★
That's right!

 ★      ★  ★    ★
I know that Jesus loves me much.

   ★
Amen!

  ★     ★     ★    ★
By name He knows me; calls me. Yes!

   ★
That's right!

# Dear Jesus,

Prayer suggestion: Make up your own clapping prayer to Jesus.

*I saw the Holy City.*
Revelation 21:1–4

# Home Sweet Home

Imagine all the different places you could live, then play this word game. Just fill in the blanks.

- The tallest place to live would be _____ . I'd like to live up there because _____ .
- The hottest place to live would be _____ . I'd like to live there because _____ .
- The most fun place to live would be _____ . I'd like to live there because _____ .

Someday everyone who knows and loves Jesus will live with Him in heaven. We don't know very much about that place, but it will be better than a tree house, a castle, or a houseboat.

God's people have been hearing about heaven for many years. You can learn what they heard by reading about heaven in the Bible. Even people long ago wanted to go to heaven.

# Dear Jesus,

Sometimes I think about heaven. What I don't understand is _____ . I know, though, that You will be in heaven with me. Amen.

159

*We are called God's children.*
1 John 3:1a

## Smile Time

What makes you happier—giving a present or getting a present? Why?

What makes you happier—Easter or your birthday? Why?

What makes you happier—getting new shoes or new clothes? Why? Show how you smile.

There are many times we can be very, very happy. Those times can be wonderful. Sometimes we expect to be happy. Sometimes we just smile right away. Can you smile now? Smile! God loves you!

## Dear Jesus,

Prayer suggestion: Talk to Jesus about a time when you were very happy.

*I am writing this to you*
*so that you may know that you have*
*eternal life.* 1 John 5:11–13.

# Writing a Book

"Mommy, why do you always sit at the typewriter?" Angela asked.

"Because I have a big job to do," her mother said. "I have to write a book."

"We can get books from the library," Angela said.

"You're right," her mother laughed. "But this is a special job for me. Typing this book is one of the most important things I will do in my whole life."

"It doesn't seem so special," Angela said. "You sure throw away a lot of papers."

"That's because I want each page to be very good," her mother said. "In my book I want to help children learn about Jesus. That's very important to me."

Jesus is very important to Angela's mother. She wants you to know how much Jesus loves you, that He cares for you, and how special you are as a child of God.

That's why Angela's mother sat at the typewriter so much. She wrote this book about Jesus for you.

You can tell other people about Jesus, too. It's exciting work. It's also a very important job.

# Dear Jesus,

I can't preach a sermon yet, but I can still tell my friends about You.

I can't write a book yet, but I can sing songs about You.

I can't build a church yet, but I can bring a friend to church. I can be a good helper, Jesus, right now! Amen.

*He spreads snow like a blanket.*
Psalm 147:16–17

# *An Ice Day*

It's been summer for several months now. Are you getting tired of the hot weather? Amy is—and she's bored. She wants to play outside, but it's too hot. She's tired of playing inside. What can she do? (What do you do when you're bored on hot summer days?)

"Amy, don't just sit around the house again today," her mother said. "Do something."

"What?" asked Amy.

"I have an idea," said her mother. "Put on your swimsuit and come into the backyard."

When Amy raced for her suit, she heard her mother take ice cubes from the freezer. (What might her mother be doing?)

In the backyard Amy's mother dumped lots of ice cubes into the cooler, then cut open a big plastic bag and laid it on the grass.

"Why don't you make an ice castle?" her mother suggested. "Use all the cubes you'd like."

Amy sat in the middle of the plastic, surrounded by the cold, slippery ice. It was hard getting the castle finished before the ice melted, but she surely had a great time.

At bedtime Amy prayed, "Thank You, God, for mommies and daddies, grandmas and grandpas, and everybody else who has such good ideas. Amen."

# *Dear Jesus,*

Prayer suggestion: Thank Jesus for the people who give you good ideas.

*From Paul . . . to the church of
God.* 1 Corinthians 1:1–3

# Thinking of You

"Why do you write so many letters to people?" Josephine asked her mother.

"Because I miss them," her mother said. "I like them to know what I'm doing, and I like to hear what my friends are doing, too. And I save their letters in a box. Then, when I feel lonely, I reread those letters, and I feel better.

"Nobody ever sends me a letter," Josephine said.

"Not yet," Mother said; "but you do have some real letters—here in the Bible."

"Letters in the Bible?" Josephine asked.

"That's right," her mother said. "Look, here's a letter that a man named Paul wrote to people in a town named Corinth. And here's a letter he sent to his friends in another town."

Ask someone to show you the different parts of the Bible. Can you find letters that people wrote to each other?

The Bible is sort of like God's love letter to us. The Bible isn't just to save, but to read—again and again.

And prayer is sort of like our love letter back to God. Ask the person reading this to write your letter to God today.

# Dear Jesus,

_____

_____ . Amen.

*Be thankful. . . .*
Colossians 3:15–17

## *Box City*

"Grandma, Grandma! Look what Josie's daddy just brought over," N. J. said excitedly. "This is going to be great."

When Grandma looked out the window, all she saw was a box here, a box there, and boxes everywhere.

"Josie's dad is cleaning out the office, and he's letting us have the boxes," N. J. said. "We're making a city."

Outside, N. J.'s friend, Josie, said, "I'll make a furniture store. I can bring out pillows for the furniture."

"I'll make a restaurant," another friend said. "We'll serve all kinds of cereal."

Every child had an idea, except N. J. What else did a city need? Then he thought of something. "I'll make the church," N. J. said. "It will be the happiest place in town."

What do you think N. J. will do to make his box look like a church? Is your church one of the happiest places in your town?

## *Dear Jesus,*

Thank You for giving me a place to live, places to shop, and a place to come and sing songs about You. I like to go to church because
_____ . Amen.

*I am going to cause food to rain
down from the sky.* Exodus 16:4a

# A Liquid Lunch

"What do you want for lunch, Jake?" his dad asked.

"It's too hot to eat," Jake answered. (Fan yourself to keep cool like Jake did.)

"It is hot," his dad said. "But our bodies need lots of liquids these days. Let's just drink some lunch."

"Drink lunch?" Jake wasn't sure he had heard correctly.

"Sure," his dad said. "Let's go to the garden and pick a nice green pepper and a couple tomatoes." (Show how you would carefully pick a tomato.)

Back inside the house Jake's dad got busy washing the vegetables. (Pretend you are washing the green pepper.)

"Aw, you're just fixing a salad," Jake said. He was disappointed. He thought dad would make lettuce juice.

"I was teasing a little," Dad said, "but we will be eating lots of liquids. Lettuce is made mostly of water. Carrots too are filled with watery juice." (How would you pull a carrot out of the ground?)

"Carrots don't feel juicy," Jake said. "They're chompy."

"Carrots are hard because they're built of a bunch of little boxes called cells. The cell walls are crunchy fibers that hold the carrot together," his dad said. "Each little box is filled with juicy liquid."

"I'm getting hungry," said Jake. "Let's thank God for this liquid lunch—and then let's eat!"

What foods have helped you keep cool this summer? Can you serve a "liquid lunch" with foods different from those Jake enjoyed?

# Dear Jesus,

Thank You for foods and drinks that help cool us this summer. I really like _____ . Amen.

*We will tell the next
generation about the Lord's power
and His great deeds.* Psalm 78:1–4

# A Bible Bookworm

"Girls, you aren't well enough to get out of bed yet," Mother said. "I want you to stay quiet again today. But today you are well enough to make a Bible bookworm."

"A Bible bookworm?" they asked together. "What's that?"

"Take turns telling each other Bible stories," Mother explained. "I'll make you a long blank bookworm out of paper."

"For every story you finish, color one section of the bookworm."

The girls settled down on the couch. Then they started telling Bible stories. The first one was Noah's Ark. (What color should they color the bookworm?)

Then they told about Queen Esther. (What color should they color the bookworm?)

Now the girls told about Jesus calming the storm. (What color should they use now?)

Now you tell a Bible story. Maybe you can start your own Bible bookworm.

# Dear Jesus,

Thank You for giving us the Bible. Amen.

*May the Lord . . . give you peace.*
2 Thessalonians 3:16

# The Shivers!

Grey was sitting in a wet swimming suit. He started to shake a bit. Grey had the shivers. (Shiver with Grey.)

Nicholas felt the wind turn cool. He was chilly. Nicholas had the shivers. (Shiver with Nicholas.)

Amelia heard a scary story. She had the shivers. (Shiver with Amelia.)

What gives you the shivers? Different things cause different people to get the shivers.

Different things make different people happy. People get sad for lots of reasons.

But knowing that Jesus cares for us can make us all smile. Knowing that Jesus will have a place for us in heaven can make each of us feel warm and cozy inside. And that's a really nice feeling, isn't it?

# Dear Jesus,

Thank You for being my Savior. Amen.

*Give thanks to the Lord!*
Isaiah 12:2–6

# Good Smells

(Sniff—or use your nose—every time you hear the word "smell" in this devotion.)

Vacation was over. Nina's family was heading home. She closed her eyes and leaned back in the car. She could still remember that last beautiful campsite.

"Remember how good breakfast *smelled* this morning?" Nina asked.

"My nose was cold," her brother said. "Breakfast *smelled* warm."

"There's nothing as good as the *smell* of coffee on the last morning of a campout," her mom said.

"Oh, yes, there is," Nina answered. "I loved our trip. But I can't wait to *smell* our house."

"*Smell* the house?" her brother laughed. "That's funny!" "But every place has a certain *smell,*" Nina said.

"Grandma's house *smells* like her powder," her dad smiled. "I love the way Aunt Gertrude's *smells* at Thanksgiving," said Nina. "I can almost taste the turkey by remembering the *smell.*"

"I like the *smell* of church at Christmas," Nina's mom said. "Church always *smells* of love and friends; but at Christmas it just seems extra special."

Nina sat quietly. She was waiting to *smell* her house. Next Sunday she would use her nose when she walked into church.

Does your church smell of love and friends? Use your nose next time you are there.

# Dear Jesus,

Thanks for my wonderful nose. Amen.

*God first loved us.*
1 John 4:19–21

# Mirror, Mirror

Pretend that you have a mirror in front of you. Hold up your hand, with your fingers together, in front of your face. Don't bump your nose!

Now look into your pretend mirror. What can you see? Are your cheeks suntanned? What color are your eyes? What else can you "see"?

Now can you see answers to these questions by looking in your mirror? What's your name? Are you friendly when you play with others? What's your favorite thing to do in the summer?

Now put your mirror down.

We can learn some things by looking into a mirror. There are other things we cannot learn by seeing a reflection.

One thing that does not show up in a mirror is the love of God that is all around us. Although He fills us up with love, we cannot see that in a mirror. But our friends can see what love does for us. They can see that love when we share.

Other people can see God's love when we say nice things.

Maybe someone else will see God's love in us when we are forgiving.

Now hold up your mirror again and smile!

I can see how you feel about God's love.

# Dear Jesus,

Prayer suggestion: Tell God how you feel now.

*You are to go to the lost sheep.*
Matthew 10:2–10

# A Busy Dozen

Have someone help you count up to a dozen. Did you count up to 12?

That's how many helpers Jesus had when He first worked here on earth. If you had been one of those busy dozen people, what would you have done? You can read in the Bible what Jesus' helpers did.

You and I weren't one of the first 12 helpers, but we can still tell people about Jesus.

Now count as high as you can in just one minute. What a good helper you could be for Jesus if you could tell that many people about Him!

# Dear Jesus,

Prayer suggestion: How do you feel about being one of Jesus' helpers? Tell Jesus.

*Believe in the Lord Jesus.*
Acts 16:22–34

# *Let's Pretend*

"Let's pretend," Kelessie said to Danny. "I'm going to be a carpenter." (What do you think Kelessie did with her hands?)

"I'm going to be a baker," said Danny. (Do something a baker might do.)

"Now guess what I am," Kelessie said. She spread her arms wide and carefully walked with one foot behind another. (What do you think Kelessie was acting out?)

"Guess who I am now," Danny said. He started to sing "Jesus Loves Me." (Whom was Danny acting like?)

# *Dear Jesus,*

It will be a while before I get a job, but I like to think about what work I might do. I know that I can already do one job for You: tell my friends about You. Amen.

*Ask, and you will receive.*
Matthew 7:7–8

# Who Ever Listens to Me?

"Dad?" Regina asked.

"Uh-huh," he answered.

"Can you read a book to me, now?" Regina asked

"Uh-huh," he answered.

"Here's the book," said Regina.

"Uh-huh," he answered.

"Dad, are you listening?" Regina asked. "Don't you ever listen to me?"

"Uh-huh," he answered. Dad continued to read the newspaper.

Has something like this ever happened to you?

Sometimes people don't listen to each other. But there's someone who will always make time for you. That's Jesus. He wants to know what you feel, how you are doing, and what's important to you.

Jesus never says, "Uh-huh."

Jesus always says, "I promise to listen to you. I promise to love you."

# Dear Jesus,

Prayer suggestion: Talk to Jesus now.

*Wipe away my sins!*
Psalm 51:1–2

## Miss Jellyface

"Angela, how did you get the jelly jar down from the shelf?" asked Mother.

Angela just stared at her. She didn't have anything in her hands. There wasn't even anything in her mouth. How could her mother know she had disobeyed and reached into the jelly? (What do you think?)

"Come here, Miss Jellyface," said Mother. "We've got to get you cleaned up."

Angela ran off crying.

"You don't love me," Angela sobbed. "You're yelling at me."

That evening, when Angela's mother came to kiss her for bedtime, her mother prayed, "Jesus, I'm sorry I got so angry. Please help me be more patient with Angela."

What was Angela's prayer that night?

## Dear Jesus,

Prayer suggestion: Ask Jesus to help your family always be forgiving.

*Everything is to be received with*
*a prayer of thanks.* 1 Timothy 4:4–5

# What's in a Lunch Box?

Ned pulled his brand-new lunch box up to the kitchen counter. Packing a new lunch box was one of the best parts of starting back to school.

First he picked up something in a plastic bag. It wasn't from the refrigerator. (What do you think he packed?)

Next he took some things from the refrigerator. He packed one item quickly before it rolled off the counter. (What did he pack?)

Then he packed something else wrapped in a plastic bag. It looked delicious. (What do you think it was?)

Last of all he poured something into his Thermos. (What would you like to drink for lunch?)

Ned looked at all the things he had packed. Sandwich, fruit, a treat, and drink. "Everything's there," he thought.

Then he looked at the lid. His mother had taped a note there. She had written a new lunchtime prayer for him. That would be nice today!

A new school year, a new lunch box, even a new lunch prayer. Ned was ready for a new day.

# Dear Jesus,

Prayer suggestion: Do you say a different prayer at each meal, or do you use the same prayer for every meal? Maybe you could trade mealtime prayers with friends so you could learn lots of new ways to say, "Thank You, Jesus, for my food and the people who grow it and fix it."

*Let us go to the Lord's house.*
Psalm 122:1

## *Sunday Best*

Teddy watched as his dad rubbed and rubbed. Dad put a little more polish on the shoe, and then he rubbed some more. He turned over the shoe, then rubbed it all over with a clean cloth. (What was Teddy's daddy doing?)

"Why do you polish your shoes on Saturday nights?" Teddy asked.

"When I was a little boy, we always tried to look our best for Sunday morning," his dad said. "My folks said we should dress up to go into God's house."

"Is that why I wear Sunday pants to church?" Teddy asked.

"That's right," said his dad. "Some of the things I learned about church when I was a little boy I'm teaching you now."

"What else am I teaching you about church?" Teddy's dad asked. "You might have to think a bit, because you might not even know you're learning."

"Well, I know church is where you learn about Jesus," Teddy said. "And I know we always like to go to church."

What are *you* learning about church? about Jesus? Will you someday tell those things to your little children, too?

## *Dear Jesus,*

You are important to me. I'm glad teachers and others will help me learn more about You. Amen.

*Love one another.*
John 15:12–13

# A Letter for You

Let's pretend the mail has just come. You go to your mailbox. How do you open it? Look, there's a letter addressed to you. How does your face look when you see it?

Now pretend to open up your letter. It's postmarked "heaven." Who might have written you? The letter is signed "Jesus."

If Jesus wrote you a letter, what would He say? Jesus could say many things to you. I don't know exactly what He would say to *you,* but I know it would be signed "Love, Jesus." That's because He loves you. That's the most important message you'll ever get.

If you wrote Jesus a letter, what would you say? I know you would end it with "Love, [*your name*]."

# Dear Jesus,

You love me. I know that. You also love my friends: _____ and
_____ . You also love my family: _____ and _____ and
_____ . You love the people who live right next door: _____
_____ and _____ .
Thank You, Jesus. Amen.

*We are witnesses of everything.*
Acts 10:37–43

# It's Autumn!

"Look, look," Mary said with excitement. "The first colored leaf. It's fall, it's fall! It's really fall!"

Fall leaves are so beautiful! What color leaf do you think Mary found? What color leaves have you found?

Colored leaves are a sign that a new season is coming. Summer will soon be over. We can see that now.

We can touch the leaves. We can crunch them. We can smell the autumn leaves burning. That's real proof that fall is coming.

Some people like proof for everything. Some people even want proof that Jesus is around. But we can't reach out and touch Jesus. We can't give Him a hug. We can't say what clothes Jesus is wearing today.

But we know about Jesus. We can read about Him in the Bible.

We know Jesus cares about us. He gives us people who love us, who will pray with us.

Jesus' death on the cross for us was proof of His love for us. Easter was many months ago. But the meaning of Easter—that Jesus rose from death—is just the same at any time of year.

Jesus loves us. Jesus died for us. We know that, for sure.

# Dear Jesus,

Prayer suggestion: Say a special autumn prayer.

*We saw His star.*
Matthew 2:1–2, 9–11

## *Pick a Little Bit o' Christmas*

"It's apple picking time; it's apple picking time," Joy sang merrily as she danced around the house.

"Everybody ready?" Grandpa called. "Time to pick a little bit o' Christmas."

"I thought we were going apple picking," Joy said. "What do apples have to do with Christmas?" she asked.

"I'll tell you when we get there," Grandpa said.

What a glorious early fall day! The apples were just starting to ripen. Joy picked so many that she could hardly carry her bag.

Then Grandpa pulled out a pocket knife and cut a ripe apple across the center. "Look at the center, Joy," Grandpa said.

Joy looked carefully. She had never seen an apple cut across the middle. There was a star right in the center.

"When you pick an apple, you pick a bit o' Christmas," Grandpa explained. "Won't be long now before we'll be celebrating Jesus' birthday. Fresh apples are the first reminder that Christmas is coming."

"And some of these apples are for Christmas dessert," Grandpa added. "We'll put some in the basement until it's time to make the apple pie for Christmas day. We did that when I was a little boy, and now we do the same thing when you're a little girl."

"Maybe I'll take my little children to pick a bit o' Christmas when I grow up," said Joy.

Try cutting an apple across as Joy's grandpa did. Do you see a reminder of the Star of Bethlehem?

## *Dear Jesus,*

Thank You for the Christmas reminder hidden in apples. Such a surprise! But I know Your love isn't a surprise. Thank You. Amen.

*My help will come from the Lord.*
Psalm 121:1–2

# A Sad September?

The sun was shining. The weather was warm. The children in the backyard were all having a wonderful time. All except Rufus.

Rufus was not happy. Rufus always got sad around this time of year. (Can you think of why Rufus was unhappy?)

September meant there would be changes. There would be fewer days like this to play outside. He would be inside the school building. He wouldn't even get to see some of his favorite friends, because they went to a different school.

Rufus felt like cutting off the rest of the calendar hanging on the kitchen wall. That way, time would just stop with today.

Would that work? What would you say to cheer up Rufus?

# Dear Jesus,

On good days, I don't want the clock to move. On bad days, time seems to go so slowly. But whatever kind of day it is, I know You are with me. I want to thank You for one special thing that happened recently: _____

_____ . I know You love me,

Jesus. Amen.

*You were eternally God, and
will be God forever.* Psalm 90:1–2

# Long Ago

"Did you have a good birthday?" Wally asked his grandma.

"Oh, yes; it was wonderful," his grandmother said. "But now it's time for you to go to sleep."

"Grandma, tell me what it was like when you were a little girl," Wally asked.

"Well, Wally, we didn't have televisions or computers when I was growing up," his grandma said.

"How did you live?" Wally asked.

"Oh, we managed very well," his grandmother laughed. "We read lots of books instead of watching TV. And I worked math problems on paper instead of a calculator."

"Wow," said Wally. "That's really different."

"Something was the same, though," Grandma said. "We prayed to the same Jesus you pray to every night. We folded our hands just as you do. And we thanked God for all His blessings."

Ask an older person what it was like when he or she grew up. What kind of clothes did they wear to church? What kind of songs did they sing? Can you pretend to have an old-fashioned church service?

# Dear Jesus,

Thank You for being there to help people I love when they were little. Thank You for watching over me now. Amen.

*The rainbow appears.*
Genesis 9:12–17

## Happy Rainbow Day!

Kent looked out the window. He couldn't wait for the rain to stop. Little drops still came down, so he couldn't go out to play, yet.

Then he sat up quickly. Something else was happening!

"Aunt Ina, come quick," Kent called. A pale band of colors appeared in the sky.

"That's neat, Kent," Aunt Ina said. The colors were so faded that the rainbow was hard to see. They both watched for a few minutes.

"It's gone," Kent said sadly. "And now it's raining even harder!"

"That's alright," Aunt Ina said. "Why don't you make a rainbow inside. That could cheer you up."

"I don't know how," Kent said sadly.

Aunt Ina looked around the room. She began collecting little cars and trucks. First she lined up all the red vehicles, then the orange, then yellow.

"Oh, what fun!" said Kent as his aunt finished the toy rainbow. Later that day Kent cut up old magazines and made rainbows from the colored pictures. When the rain stopped, he made rainbows on the sidewalk with colored chalk.

How can you have a rainbow day?

## Dear God,

Thank You for sending the first rainbow to Noah. When I see a rainbow, I think of Your promise to take care of me. Amen.

*His love is eternal.*
Psalm 136:1

# Cooking Time

Renee was going to help her mother cook supper. It was her very first time at really helping.

"Renee, cooking is very exciting," her mother said. "Tonight you'll see some of our foods get bigger after cooking, and some get smaller."

That's funny, Renee thought. She washed her hands and took some ground meat. She copied her mother as she made a hamburger patty. (Would that get bigger or smaller after it was cooked?)

Next Renee washed some spinach leaves. She stuffed them into a very large pot, but the lid hardly fit. If that got bigger after cooking, it would go all over the kitchen, Renee thought. (What happens to spinach while it cooks?)

Renee and her mother then pulled off the husks from corn on the cob. Renee wondered: What would happen to that while it cooked?

"Turn on the oven light, Renee," her mother said. "How is the bread doing?"

"It's growing," Renee said.

"And so are you," her mother said as she hugged her. "You are a real help in the kitchen. On days like this I am so grateful God gave you to me to be my daughter," her mother said. "Jesus and I will always love you, Honey. I want you to remember that."

You, too, are growing up. You are able to do new things. But no matter how much you grow or change, Jesus will always love you, too.

# Dear Jesus,

I never get tired of hearing that people love me. I know You love me, too. Amen.

*My heart praises the Lord.*
Luke 1:46–55

# A Singin' Saturday

"Get the rake, Mindy Sue," Dad called. "We've got lots of leaves over here."

Mindy Sue started raking. But, oh, did she frown.

"Mindy Sue, hold this ladder while I clean out the gutter," Mom said.

Mindy Sue steadied the ladder. But, oh, did she frown.

"Mindy Sue, clean out this toy box in the garage," Dad said.

Now Mindy Sue was really frowning.

But then Mindy Sue started to smile. (Can you guess why?)

Mom brought out a tape recorder. The first song was "Silent Night." The whole family, except Mindy Sue, started singing. (Can you hum "Silent Night"?)

The next song was "Angels We Have Heard on High." Mindy Sue frowned again—until the family started singing the long "Gloria." (Do you remember how that goes?) Finally, Mindy Sue smiled.

Sing with Mindy Sue—and smile just like Mindy Sue:

"Gloria, in Excelsis Deo!
Gloria, in Excelsis Deo."

It doesn't have to be Christmas to remember the birth of Jesus.

# Dear Jesus,

Prayer suggestion: Sing another of your favorite Christmas songs for your prayer to Jesus.

*Your sins are forgiven for
the sake of Christ.* 1 John 2:12

# I Forgive You

Donna looked sadly at her sweater. The brand-new school sweater
didn't look new anymore. Next time she'd try to remember to bring it
in from the playground. But now she was worried; what would her
mother say? (What do you think might happen?)

"Mommy," Donna called, "I'm home."

"How was school, Honey?"

"Fine," Donna said. "Something happened to my sweater, but I
can still use it."

"Your new sweater?" her mother asked. "What could have happened? It's not even raining or muddy outside."

Donna held it up. The sweater had dirty footprints all over it, and
it was very wrinkled. (What had happened to it?)

"Well, at least you brought it home," her mother said. "Accidents
happen. I'll scrub it right away. Please get the soap. You can help."

"Sure," Donna said with relief. (Show how Donna scrubbed the
sweater.)

How do you think Donna felt when Donna's mother forgave her for
damaging the new sweater?

The relief and happiness Donna felt at not being punished is just a
little bit like how we can feel with Jesus' forgiveness. He will always
forgive us no matter what kind of mistakes we make. Jesus will always
have His arms open to us with the message, "Come here; tell Me what
happened; of course I forgive you."

# Dear Jesus,

Thank You for forgiving me when I do things that aren't right. Help
me learn to forgive others. Amen.

*I will bless the person who puts his*
*trust in Me.* Jeremiah 17:7–8

# A Leaf Hunt

It's fall, it's fall! Soon the weather will be changing. A new season is coming.

Can you go on a leaf hunt? Soon leaves will be covering the ground in some areas. Are there leaves around your house? Where? You can go outside and look.

Where do you think leaves might be hiding? Under a bush? Blown against the corner with the garbage cans?

How many fall leaves can you find?

Some people say that God paints the world in color during fall. What are your favorite fall colors?

# Dear Jesus,

I think Your world is colorful in all seasons. In spring the grass is yellow-green. In summer the sky is blue. Now that it's nearing fall, I see more colors. They are _____ . In winter the color I see most is _____ . Thanks, Jesus, for Your colorful world. Amen.

*All of God's people send you*
*their greetings.*
2 Corinthians 13:11–14

# Hello and Good-bye

Renee looked back sadly at the farm. She wouldn't be back to visit the animals until next spring.

She listened to the "cluck, cluck, cluck." (What animal was Renee hearing?)

She looked back toward the animal that had been so cute and cuddly last spring. Now it was almost grown up. (What animal did she see?)

Renee was going to miss the big horse most of all. Today she had picked a fresh, ripe apple from the tree. The horse had taken it right from her hand! Now the big animal stood by the fence, switching its tail.

"Look, Renee, the horse you like is waving good-bye with its tail," her father said.

Renee sat glumly in the car. All the way home she remembered the wonderful summer times at the farm. (What do you think she had liked best of all?)

When they got home, Renee walked slowly into the house. There was her cat, Princess, waving her tail. "Meow, meow," she purred.

"Well, look at that," her dad said. "Princess is saying hello with her tail."

"I like hellos better than good-byes," Renee said. "Good-bye is such a sad thing."

"It's not sad when you're waving to me and you're off to the zoo," said her dad. "Now, let's get supper."

When is a good-bye happy for you?

# Dear Jesus,

Some good-byes really make me feel sad. When I feel like that, help me remember I can talk to You. Amen.

*The wind blows . . . but you
do not know where it comes from or
where it is going.* John 3:5–8

## *Jesus Is Near*

Here's a wind game to play.

Blow in. Blow out. Now lick your finger. Now blow it. Can you feel the wind you made?

Sometimes it takes a wet finger to feel the wind. Moving air is all around us, even if we can't always feel it.

Jesus is like the wind, in some ways. He is always around us, even though we can't see Him.

You can make a "Jesus wind strip." Cut pieces of yarn. Tie them onto a hanger. Then hang your wind strip where you can see it at night.

If you're ever scared at bedtime, or if you can't go to sleep, blow the air around the wind strip. That can remind you that Jesus is always with you.

You are never alone, not even when you sleep. Jesus is with you, always.

## *Dear Jesus,*

Prayer suggestion: Pray to Jesus your favorite prayer.

*A worm attacked the plant.*
Jonah 4:5–7

# The Wiggly, Squiggly Ones

"It's only drizzling now," Frank's mother said. "Go out and play under an umbrella."

"Yuck, Mommy," said Frank. "There are wiggly, squiggly worms all over the sidewalk."

"Oh, Frank," his mother said. "Let's go outside and look."

(What did Frank and his mother put on to go out in the drizzle?)

"It even smells like worms," Frank said once they got outdoors.

"Frank, a worm is an amazing little animal," his mother said. "Look what this worm is doing now."

(What do you think the worm did?)

"Maybe he'll climb up on this stick," his mother said.

"Be careful you don't break his bones," Frank said.

"A worm doesn't have any bones, Frank," his mother said. "No bones, no eyes, no ears to hear, either."

"I told you worms were yucky," Frank said.

"I think they're amazing," his mother said. "Most of all, worms are God's creatures."

What are some other animals that go outside in the rain?

# Dear Jesus,

I never knew much about worms. There's even a worm story in the Bible. I love learning about the animals You created. Amen.

*I . . . give you the harvest*
*season each year*. Jeremiah 5:24b

# The Smell of September

Julie could smell it was autumn. (What do you smell in fall?)

Just yesterday at Julie's house the air smelled damp. (Can you guess what the weather was like?)

Today Julie is smelling smoke. (What do you think could be burning?)

Julie can also touch autumn. When she walks down the sidewalk, something crunches under her feet. (What do you think she's crunching?)

Julie loves the smell and touch of autumn.

What are you doing at your house this fall?

# Dear Jesus,

Thank You for the different times of year. The thing I like best about fall is _____ . Amen.

*I will lead My blind people.*
Isaiah 42:16

# A Look Through Julie's Eyes

Do you remember Julie? Yesterday we talked about autumn at her house. We talked about things that you and Julie feel and smell in autumn.

Now, use your eyes. Look out a window. How can you tell it's autumn? Just use your eyes.

Julie can't see the same signs of autumn. She is blind. Spring, summer, fall, and winter all look the same to Julie. She can only see a few shadows through her eyes.

Julie uses her ears, her nose, and her hands to learn about things like fall. She learned about Jesus that way, too.

Julie has a friend who tells her stories from the Bible. Julie listens to the words at church. And you should hear Julie sing about Jesus!

Julie can't look at a church and know that it is a place to learn about Jesus. Julie can't see the pretty windows at church that make the sunlight look so colorful.

But Julie knows Jesus loves her. Julie knows Jesus will take care of her in spring, summer, fall, and winter. Julie feels so good about that!

How do you feel hearing about Julie and Jesus?

# Dear Jesus,

Thank You for my wonderful body. Amen.

*To Jesus Christ be the glory
and power forever.*
Revelation 1:4–6

# A Good Question

"Did Jesus ever eat apple pie?" Jared asked his dad.

"That's a good question," his dad said. "Go ask your mother."

"Did Jesus ever eat apple pie?" Jared asked his mother.

"That's a good question," his mother said. "Go ask your grandfather."

"Did Jesus ever eat apple pie?" Jared asked his grandfather.

"That's a good question," his grandfather said. "Go ask . . . ."

"No, Grandpa," Jared interrupted. "I can't go ask somebody else. I'll just have to ask Jesus when I get to heaven."

What will you want to ask Jesus when you get to heaven?

# Dear Jesus,

Prayer suggestion: Tell Jesus what you will ask Him when you get to heaven.

*I love the house where You live,*
*O Lord.* Psalm 26:8

# A Church Box

"But Mommy, I want to go to church," Sabrina wailed.

"I'm glad you like church," her mother said. "But you are just not quite ready to go out, yet. You need one more day inside, just to be sure that your cold is gone."

"I have to go to church," Sabrina insisted, "It's just not Sunday without church."

"I'm sorry, Sabrina," her mother said firmly. "You can go next week, but not today."

Sabrina sat sadly and looked out the window. It didn't seem like Sunday. She wouldn't hear the pretty music. She couldn't visit with her friends. She couldn't hear about Jesus.

Then Sabrina had an idea.

"Mom, do you have an extra box?" Sabrina asked. "It needs to be pretty big."

"There's an empty box in the front closet that you may have," her mother answered. "Why do you need it?"

"You'll see," Sabrina said. (What do you think Sabrina will do with the box?)

Sabrina was busy for a long time. She used scissors, crayons, and paper.

When her mother peeked around the door, this is what she saw: Sabrina had made the box into a church! Her dolls were all sitting nicely, listening to Sabrina talk about Jesus.

Can you make a church box, too?

# Dear Jesus,

Thank You for giving us our church. I especially like _____ . Amen.

*You . . . will be God forever.*
Psalm 90:1–2

# Changes, Changes

It was autumn where Angela lived. The leaves were turning different colors.

The temperature was changing, too. The thermometer on the back porch showed it was getting cooler. (What kind of clothes would Angela wear to play outside?)

Angela's grandpa emptied the swimming pool. Angela put away the sprinkling can and hose.

New seasons bring many changes.

But Jesus stays the same in spring, summer, fall, and winter.

We can always talk to Jesus. Jesus loves us all year.

Today we start a new month. Fall is a new season. But Jesus is still your best Friend.

# Dear Jesus,

It's autumn where I live. I like this season because _____
_____ .

Thank You for giving us a new season. Thank You for staying the same. Amen.

*Love one another.* 1 John 4:7

# Love, Love, Love

"I love you very, very . . ." Christina told Aunt Ruth.

Christina was trying to tell Aunt Ruth how much she loved her. Who are people you love? Show one person, right now, that you love him or her.

Did you show love by smiling? When you were a baby, that was the first way you showed love.

Did you show love with a hug or kiss? It feels good to be close to somebody.

Did you tell someone you loved him or her? It's nice to hear, "I love you."

That's what Jesus says when He gives us people who help us grow. Jesus says that, too, when He gives us people who can love us.

Jesus loves each of us "very, very . . ." Oops, I forgot a word. Fill it in for me: Jesus loves me very, very, _____ .

# Dear Jesus,

Thank You for loving me. I love You, too. And thank You for giving me people who help me grow and who love me. Their names are _____ . I love them, too. Amen.

*This child is chosen by God.*
Luke 2:25–35

# Move Over, Baby

We have a baby at our house.

His name is Matthew. Today Matthew is five months old. How old are you?

Matthew learned to smile a few months ago. How do you smile? Last month he learned to put his hands together. Can you hold your hands together?

Now Matthew is rolling over. How do you roll over?

Soon Matthew will learn to crawl. You are probably good at crawling. Crawl a little bit, the way you did when you were a baby. Now crawl back to this book.

Soon, too, Matthew will learn about Jesus. What should we tell baby Matthew about Jesus?

# Dear Jesus,

When I was a baby, I didn't know about You. But You loved me, anyway. When I was little, I couldn't walk or talk, or even smile. Now I can do many things. I can _____

_____ . Also, I now know that

You love me and _____

_____ . Amen.

*Even the hairs of your head have
all been counted.* Matthew 10:29–31

# *Who Knows It All?*

Use your fingers to show the answers:

- How many noses do you have?
- How many ears do you have?
- How many fingers do you have?
- How many hairs do you have on your head?

That last questions is hard to answer. Not even grown-ups can tell how many hairs are on their head.

But God knows. God knows all about you. God knows you have one nose, two ears, and ten fingers. In the Bible, Jesus says that God even knows how many hairs are on your head.

God also knows He loves you.

What do you know about God? There are lots of things we might know about God, but one thing is most important: He loves us.

# *Dear God,*

Thank You for knowing all about me—for knowing that I live in _____ , for knowing that I like to play with _____ , for knowing that my name is _____ , and for loving me. I _____ You, too. Amen.

*I pray to You all day long.*
Psalm 86:3–5

# Don't Forget

It was almost bedtime. Samuel's mom helped him take off his play clothes. He wiggled into his pajamas. Samuel went to the bathroom, then brushed his teeth. It was time for listening to a book. Then the night-light blinked on.

"Good night, Samuel. I love you," said Mom as she tucked the covers around him.

"But Mommy, you forgot something," said Samuel. (What did his mother forget?)

Talking to Jesus, or praying, is something to do every day. Samuel and his mom always pray together before going to sleep at night. Some people pray before eating a meal. Some people pray when they wake up in the morning. When do you pray?

Jesus doesn't count how often you pray. He doesn't keep track of when you pray. He just wants to hear from you.

# Dear Jesus,

Prayer suggestion: Tell Jesus about your day.

*You will be witnesses for Me.*
Acts 1:8

# Witness

Let's do some pretending with sounds.

- What would one day say to another day?
- How would an alligator talk to a crocodile?
- What kind of sound would a daddy lion make to a mommy lion?
- What would you say to a friend about Jesus?

When you tell somebody about Jesus, you are being a witness. *Witness* is a big word. Witness is an important word. Telling people about how much Jesus loves them is one of the things we are supposed to do.

You can be a witness. You can tell somebody about Jesus.

# Dear Jesus,

I didn't know I could be a witness. That's a big word, though. Mostly I just want to tell people about You. I know one person I can tell about You. I can tell _____ . Amen.

*Jesus wept.* John 11:32–36

# About Dying

Scott was angry. His grandpa had died.

"Now Grandpa can't take me fishing next summer," thought Scott. How would you feel if someone died?

Some people feel guilty (even though they aren't). How do you know when someone feels guilty?

Some people get sad. How do you know when someone is sad?

Some people get lonesome. What do you do when you're lonesome?

We can tell Jesus how we feel. He wants to know when we hurt inside.

# Dear Jesus,

Prayer suggestion: Do you know someone who died? Are you worried about someone dying? Tell Jesus. He will know how you feel. Jesus will understand.

*Let us go to the*
*Lord's house.* Psalm 122:1

# Where Am I?

Let's try some riddles about buildings:
● I am a place where you buy things.
You buy food here.
I am _____
● I am a place you visit when you are sick.
You come here when you don't feel well.
I am _____
● I am a place where you get money.
You can drive to me, walk to me, or come inside me.
I am _____
● I am a place where you learn about Jesus.
You see your friends when you come here.
I am _____

There are lots of things inside a church building. You might sit on a pew or chair at church. You might hear beautiful music. You might look through pretty glass windows.

But the best thing about church isn't the building. Can you guess what is best?

You come to hear about Jesus. That's what's most important about a church.

# Dear Jesus,

I'm glad there is a place I can go to learn more about You. Amen.

*Join with us in*
*the fellowship.* 1 John 1:3

## *Circles*

Make a circle with your fingers.
Make a circle with your arms.

Now ask someone to make a circle around you. Who is in the center of the circle? When you're in the center of a circle, you feel really important.

Find a picture of Jesus. Now make a circle with your fingers around the picture. You have put Jesus in the center of your circle. He is an important part of that circle.

Because you are a child of God, Jesus wants to be at the center of your life. That means that when you play, He wants you to act as His child. When someone asks for help, He wants you to act as He would. He wants to be important in your life.

We can't go around holding our fingers in a circle in order to remember that Jesus is at the center of our lives. But we can try to do things like a child of God.

## *Dear Jesus,*

I try to remember to act like Your child. I am kind to people in my family and to my friends. I try to share. I also _____
_____ . Amen.

*While we were still sinners . . . Christ*
*died for us!*
Romans 5:8

# It's Not Fair

"It's just not fair," Debbie told her mommy. "Kristin gets to go to a party and I don't."

"It's just not fair," Tom told his dad. "David is going on vacation. We never go anywhere."

"It's just not fair," Megan said to Muneeza on the playground. "Teacher always sends Mark on errands just because he gets done so fast with his schoolwork."

Have you ever said, "It's not fair"?

Do you think it's fair that Jesus loves us? We all do wrong. At some time each of us has acted poorly. There are times we don't do what we should. But Jesus doesn't punish us. He forgives us.

It's just not fair that Jesus loves us even though we do bad things. It's not fair, but it's true.

No matter what we do, no matter how we act, Jesus still loves us.

# Dear Jesus,

Thanks for everything. Amen.

*There is a boy here. . . .*
John 6:5–13

# Not Too Little

''You're too little.''

How do you feel when someone says that to you? You are too young to drive a car, to bake a cake all by yourself, or to use the lawn mower.

But you aren't too little for some things. What are some things you are good at doing? _____

There's another thing you aren't too little for: being God's child. How old are you? _____That's certainly old enough to be loved by Jesus.

Now, think. Whom can you tell about Jesus? What can you say about Jesus?

You're not too little for Jesus. You're just right.

# Dear Jesus,

You know how old I am. You know that I am _____years old. That is old enough to be Your helper. Being Your helper makes me feel _____ . Amen.

*The new has come.*
2 Corinthians 5:17

# Something New

[After every statement with a ★ ask your child to show with a sad or a happy face how he or she feels.]

Albert was so excited. He was going to get new shoes.★ But the first day Albert wore the shoes, they made his feet hurt.★

Nicholas was getting a new Sunday school teacher.★ But Nicholas liked his other teacher.★

Luis was moving to a brand-new house.★ But Luis liked his old house.★

Blake's new baby sister was coming home from the hospital.★ Blake wasn't sure how he felt.★

It might be fun to get something new. It can be exciting or scary, too.

# Dear Jesus,

Prayer suggestion: Talk to Jesus about a time when you had something new. He always wants to know how you feel.

---

*These have been written.*
John 20:30–31

# Dress-Up

It is almost Halloween. Joe and Lisa are going to dress up like their favorite Bible people this year.

With his costume Joe needs two cats, two dogs, two birds, and a boat. Whom do you think Joe is dressing like? [Noah]

Lisa is looking for a beautiful crown and colored scarves to tie around her. Whom is Lisa going to dress like? [Esther]

If you could dress up like your favorite Bible person, what would you wear?

# Dear Jesus,

It's fun to think about a time long ago when You were a little boy. One of the people I like to hear about in the Bible is _____ . Even though I like that person, You will always be the most important person in the Bible. Amen.

*Your Word is a lamp*
*to guide me.* Psalm 119:105

# *A Job for Jesus*

Whom do you know who works in an office? who works in a school? Do you know someone who works outdoors?

Many people go to school to learn about their job. They study and practice what they will be doing.

You are learning about your work as you go through the pages of this book. Your job is for Jesus. That's why words about Jesus are on every page. What do you know about Jesus?

# *Dear Jesus,*

I know lots of things about You. I know You love me. I still want to learn this about You: _____ .

I can find some answers in Your Book, the Bible. Thanks for giving me the important job of being Your helper. Amen.

*Your love . . . will always*
*keep me safe.* Psalm 40:11

# Just Plain Me

Jennifer and Gregory were talking about Halloween. Jennifer was so excited! She was going to wear a clown costume.

Gregory was not excited. He didn't even want to wear a costume.

"Mommy, I don't want to be a scarecrow," said Greg. "Birds will come and peck me."

"Greg, you will still be yourself on Halloween," said Mom.

"Mommy, I don't want to be a lion, either," said Greg. "People will think I bite."

"Greg, You will just wear a costume." said Mom. "All that will be different will be your clothes. You'll still be my little boy."

"After Halloween, when I take off the costume, will I be me again?" Greg asked.

"Greg, you'll be you however you dress on Halloween," she said. "You can even dress like my little boy."

# Dear Jesus,

Help me remember that You love me just the way I am. You will always love me—no matter what I wear, no matter what I do. You will always love me. Amen.

*Each of you must put aside
some money.* 1 Corinthians 16:2

## Money to Give Away

"Money, money, money. I like money," said Samantha as she sat with her teddy bear bank. "I like to feel the paper money. It's soft. And the coins go clink, clink, clink."

What do you think Samantha will do with her money?

Samantha gave some of her money to God. She couldn't hand it to Jesus, but she took it to church. The church was going to use her money to print a newspaper about Jesus. What other ways could a church use money?

Next time Samantha plays with her teddy bear bank, she will count out some more money to give to church. Samantha likes to do that.

Why do you think giving money to church makes her happy?

## Dear Jesus,

Thank You for giving me money that I can save and spend. I know that when I take money to church, I help other people learn about You. Amen.

*Rejoice!* Philippians 4:4

## Laugh a Lot

Michelle clomped into her daddy's room.

"See, I got my shoes and socks on all by myself," she said.

"That's nice, but the shoes are on the wrong feet," Daddy answered.

"Are the socks on the right feet?" Michelle asked.

Why was Michelle's question funny?

When did you laugh today?

Jesus wants us to be happy and to have good times. Tell Jesus about a time you smiled.

## Dear Jesus,

I don't always smile. But I want to tell You about a time when I had fun: _____ . Amen.

*I am the vine, and you are the branches.* John 15:4–7

# Lost and Found

John lost a puzzle piece. How do you think John feels?

Mickey can't find the dollar bill he got for Christmas. How do you think Mickey feels?

But, wait! John found the puzzle piece under his bed. And look! Mickey's money was stuck in a book.

What kind of look do these boys have on their faces now?

Every day we feel lots of different ways. Jesus wants to know how we feel. He cares about how we feel. Tell Jesus about your feelings today.

# Dear Jesus,

Today I felt _____ when _____ .

Sometimes I feel sad when _____ .

It makes me happy, though, to know that You love me. No matter how I feel, I can always feel good inside because You're smiling at me. That's a warm, friendly feeling, Jesus. Amen.

*Hide me in the shadow of*
*Your wings.* Psalm 17:8

# No Witches! No Ghosts!

Can you believe Halloween is almost here? What will be the most fun?

It's the day before Halloween at Benjamin's house. But Benjamin doesn't have a smile on his face.

"Ben, what's the matter?" asked his mom.

"Nothing," said Ben.

"Benjamin, something must be bothering you," she said.

"Nothing's wrong. But don't look up in the sky tomorrow, Mommy," said Ben.

"Why, Ben?" asked his mom.

"You might see a ghost or goblin," said Ben. "I'm not going to look up because a witch might be flying around on a broom. Jerry and Ted said so."

"Oh, Ben," said his mom. "The boys were just teasing. You know there are no real witches or ghosts or goblins."

"Really? Oh, really?" said Ben. "Oh, wow! I can't wait until tomorrow. It's Halloween!"

# Dear Jesus,

I get scared, sometimes. Sometimes I'm afraid of _____ .

Please help me remember, Jesus, that I can always tell You what is scary. I know You'll listen. Amen.

*Listen! I stand at the door
and knock.* Revelation 3:20–21

## *Knock, Knock*

"Ring, ring." Another trick-or-treater was at the door. It was a busy night at Aretha's house.

"Who are you, really?" Aretha asked the costumed person.

"I'll give you a clue," said the voice behind the mask. "I'm family."

"Oh, Jimmy, Jimmy, I know your voice," Aretha said happily as her cousin took off the mask.

If Jesus stood at your door and knocked, He might say much the same thing. "You're family," He might say. You're part of His family. He loves you.

## *Dear Jesus,*

Prayer suggestion: Tell Jesus now how you feel about Him.

*We have found the Messiah.*
John 1:40–42

# Shout It Out

Show how you can jump like a kangaroo.
Now sing like a bird.
Can you wag your tail like a dog?
Have you ever felt like a turtle with its head inside the shell?
Sometimes it feels good to be all alone. Name a time you wanted to hide.

Did you ever feel like hiding when somebody asked you about Jesus? I hope not. I hope you wanted to tell them how much Jesus loves you.

Sing like a bird when you answer this question: ''Who is Jesus?''

Roar like a lion to answer this: ''Whom does Jesus love?''

Do people understand what you said when you sang like a bird or roared like a lion?

This time, talk like you usually talk and answer this question: ''What's important about Jesus?''

# Dear Jesus,

Help me tell other people about You. Amen.

*Have your sins washed away.*
Acts 22:16

# *Cleaning Up*

What can you wash with a rag and a bucket of water?
What can you clean with some soap and water?
What room in your house needs some cleaning right now?
Churches need cleaning, too. Who cleans your church? Do you know who wipes off the Sunday school chalkboard? Have you ever seen someone wash the church windows?
What's your favorite thing to clean?

# *Dear Jesus,*

Thanks for water. I like to play in it. I like to splash in it. I like to

_____ .

Water helps us keep things clean, too. Thanks, Jesus, for water. Amen.

*In His Word I trust.*
Psalm 130:5–6

# Extra Thanks

Bill was so excited! He was getting a new wheelchair. His arms got very tired moving the wheels of his old chair. Maybe it was because he went so many places so fast.

Bill loved to bounce balls on the playgound. And when his friends played kickball, Bill would kick the ball with the side of the chair. But now he was getting a chair that moved with the touch of a switch. And it was coming today!

Bill hung around the house all day. By suppertime the delivery truck still hadn't come. Bill and his mother looked at the order. The date was for next week. Seven more days to wait.

Sunday, Monday, Tuesday, Wednesday—the week was going so slowly! Finally, it was a week later. Bill was afraid the new chair wouldn't come, so he wheeled off to play with a friend.

When he rolled home for lunch, a large packing crate was sitting empty, next to the garbage can.

Bill could feel his heart thumping. There, inside the kitchen, was the new wheelchair.

Bill was so excited that when he finally zoomed to the table for lunch he added some extra words to the mealtime prayer.

What do think Bill told Jesus?

# Dear Jesus,

Sometimes I forget to thank You for little things that are really important. Thanks, Jesus for _____
_____ . Amen.

*The old things have
disappeared.* Revelation 21:3–4

## *Look Ahead!*

"Guess what I'm going to be next Halloween," Kimiko said.

"Why, Kimiko, we just had this Halloween," her grandmother answered.

"I know; but guess what I'm going to be next Halloween," Kimiko repeated.

Are you looking forward to next Halloween, too? It's fun to think ahead. Are you eager for Christmas to come?

We look forward to things we enjoy. We all look forward to being in heaven with Jesus. In heaven no one will get sick or be afraid. No one will cry. Best of all, we will live with Jesus and be able to see Him.

## *Dear Jesus,*

Prayer suggestion: Talk to Jesus about heaven.

*Respect your father and
your mother.* Exodus 20:12

# Helping Each Other

"Rachel, time to clean up your room," said Daddy.

"But Daddy, it's too much room," answered Rachel.

"It's time to clean it up, Rachel," he said again.

"I'm too tired," said Rachel. "And besides, it's too messy to clean up all by myself."

"I didn't want to stop what I was doing yesterday and drive you to that birthday party," Daddy reminded her. "But we need to help each other."

Who are some people God gives to help you?

# Dear Jesus,

Thank You for giving me these people to love me: _____
_____ . Thank You for giving me
these people to help me grow up: _____ . Amen.

*Jesus was there alone.*
Matthew 14:22–23

# Alone Time

"Leave me alone," shouted Marsha.

"What's wrong with you?" her sister asked.

"I just want some alone time," said Marsha. "Let me be by myself."

Being alone is important for everybody. Where do you go to be alone?

When Jesus lived on earth, He liked alone time, too. He would sometimes go away by Himself to rest. Sometimes He would sleep. Sometimes He would pray. What do you do when you're alone?

# Dear Jesus,

I'm glad You understand what it is like to want to be alone. Thank You that You are always with me, even when I am alone. Amen.

*So great is His love for [them].*
Psalm 103:11–13

# Who Started It?

"He started it!"

"No, she did!"

"He did."

"She did."

Can you tell what's going on here? It's an argument.

It's not much fun to argue. It doesn't make me feel good when I disagree with someone.

It's not good to argue. But there is one good thing: Jesus will forgive us. Even if we start a disagreement, Jesus will still forgive us.

# Dear Jesus,

Thank You for always forgiving me. Amen.

*He is Jesus.* John 1:45–46

# *God's House*

Let's pretend. Imagine the most wonderful place to live in the whole wide world. Will your imaginary house have elevators? a big zoo in the backyard? toys in every room?

Think now of the place where you really live. Is there space for you to sleep? Can you look out a window? Can you sit down to eat? Those things help make a good place for a child to live.

Sometimes a church is called the house of God. A church might be a place where you feel like being quiet. A church might have a beautiful tall steeple or pretty windows. But a church doesn't need those things.

A church needs people to come and worship. A church needs you to come and learn about Jesus. A church is a place where you can bring a friend who doesn't know about Jesus. That's what makes a good house of God.

# *Dear Jesus,*

Help me remember that You like me to come to church. Help me think of someone I can bring with me to Your house, my church. Amen.

*Go, then, to all peoples*
*everywhere.* Matthew 28:19–20

# Calling You!

Jeremy knows it's suppertime when his grandfather calls, "Come and get it."

Abby comes for supper when she hears, "Soup's on."

Wanda runs to the kitchen when her stomach growls.

Who calls you for mealtime?

God calls us, too. He doesn't call us when it's time for a hamburger. No, He calls us for a more important reason.

God calls us to be His helpers. God wants each of us to tell other people about Jesus.

God has called you to be His helper. Now, whom can you call to tell about Jesus?

# Dear Jesus,

I know You have asked me to be Your helper. Help me when I tell other people about You. Amen.

*Let the children come to Me.*
Mark 10:13–16

# *Rain, Rain, Go Away*

"There's nothing to do," sighed Tony as he looked outside. Rain was streaming down the window. The yard looked soggy after days of wet weather.

"Read a book," said his mother.

"I don't know how to read," said Tony.

"Look at the pictures in a book," suggested his mother.

"I'm tired of all my old books," said Tony.

"Make your own book," she said. "Draw pictures about something. I'll help you put it together."

"All I know about is rain. Rain, rain, rain! That's all it ever does," Tony complained.

"Here's a leftover paper from Sunday school," Tony's mother said. "That might give you some ideas. Why don't you make a book about Jesus?"

Can you help Tony? What could he put in his book about Jesus?

# *Dear Jesus,*

Thank You for giving us the Bible so we can learn more about You. Thank You for Sunday schools and teachers. Amen.

*The greatest in the Kingdom . . .*
*becomes like this child.*
Matthew 18:1–4

# *Always God's Child*

"I want to be your baby again," said Virginia as she crawled onto her mother's lap.

Have you ever wanted to go back to being little?

Show something you did when you were a baby.

Sometimes it might seem nice to be a baby again. Being a baby means you get cuddled and held a lot. But it also means you can't do lots of things you can do now. Show one thing you couldn't do as a baby.

Soon you will be doing more and more things. But you will always be a child of God. Now point to the oldest person in the room. Even that person is still a child of God.

Even though we grow up and do lots of wonderful things, we can always be a child with God. Just as a baby is loved, so God will always love us. A baby needs lots of help. God is always ready to help us because we are His children.

We can be grown up with everybody else, but we can still be a child with God.

# *Dear Jesus,*

Thank You for loving me as Your child. I'm not a baby anymore because I can do lots of things, like _____ .

But I know You will always love me as Your child, no matter how old I get. Amen.

*Call to Me when trouble comes.*
Psalm 50:15

# *Call for Help*

Cheryl sat quietly. She knew something serious must have happened. Mommy was so quiet. Daddy looked upset. Something wasn't right.

Cheryl was worried. What could she do? Then she had an idea. Her parents always told her to talk to Jesus when she had a problem. That's what she'd suggest.

"Mommy, why don't you call God on the telephone and tell Him what's wrong?" Cheryl suggested.

"That's a good idea," her dad smiled. "But we don't have to bother with a phone call. Let's just pray."

Cheryl sat quietly while her parents prayed. Cheryl knew God would listen to their words.

# *Dear Jesus,*

Sometimes I forget to ask You for help. I get angry and forget that I can talk to You. Help me remember You are closer than a phone call. You're right here with me. Amen.

*He loved us.* 1 John 4:10

# *A Lousy Thanksgiving?*

"What a crummy day," Akeem said as he walked into the kitchen.

"Why Akeem, it's Thanksgiving. How can Thanksgiving be crummy?" asked Aunt Helen.

"It's not just crummy," Akeem answered, "it's a yucky, lousy, icky, crummy day." And he wandered off.

Have you ever felt like Akeem? What makes a bad day for you?

Some days go better than other days. That's true for everybody. Sometimes around holidays people think everything should be great for everybody. That's a nice thought, but it doesn't always work out that way. How is the Thanksgiving season for you this year?

There's always one thing that is good about every day: Jesus loves us. Jesus loves us in November, on our birthday, and even when we have a yucky, lousy, icky, crummy day.

Jesus doesn't promise us that every day will be super, but He promises to love us all the time.

# *Dear Jesus,*

Prayer suggestion: How do you feel Jesus' love today? Thank Him for that.

*Perfect love drives out*
*all fear.* 1 John 4:18

## Plenty for All

"I want a drumstick," Deron yelled across the table.

"Deron, your cousins asked for the drumsticks first," his mom reminded him. "They are our guests. You'll have to share."

"I don't want to share. There won't be enough for me," cried Deron.

How do you think Deron feels now?

Sometimes sharing doesn't seem like much fun.

There's one thing we can share and still have enough for ourselves: Jesus' love. Jesus has enough love for everybody. There's plenty to go around. Jesus will love us, and love us, and love us—and there still is plenty of love for everybody else, too.

## Dear Jesus,

Thank You for loving me all the time. Amen.

*Give thanks to the Lord.*
Psalm 136:1

## Thanksgiving Every Day

Today is a holiday at Carol's house. Today her family is celebrating Thanksgiving. But Carol doesn't feel like she's celebrating. Let's listen as she talks to her aunt:

"Aunt Rose, why don't we get presents today?"

"Because it's Thanksgiving," Carol.

"My birthday is a holiday and I get presents. We get lots of presents on Christmas. And on Valentine's Day and Halloween we get things, too. Why can't I get a Thanksgiving present?"

"On Thanksgiving we remember the presents we get the rest of the year," says Aunt Rose. "We thank God for the nice meals we eat, for the clothes we wear, for the toys we play with every day."

As Carol listens to Aunt Rose, she remembers other things that were presents to her.

## Dear Jesus,

Prayer suggestion: What can you thank God for?

*God loved us.* 1 John 4:11

# Word Games

Finish these sentences:

- Jesus loves me. Jesus loves _____ .
- Jesus forgives me. I can forgive _____ .
- A word that rhymes with boo is the word _____ .

Did you finish those word games with "you"?
*You* is an important word.
You are an important person.
God loves you. He cares about you. He gives you people to love, too.
Let's try those word games again:

- Jesus loves me. Jesus loves _____ .
- Jesus forgives me. I can forgive _____ .

Can you make up a riddle using "you"?

# Dear Jesus,

Prayer suggestion: Ask Jesus to help you love and forgive others because He loves and forgives you.

*God has blessed us.*
Psalm 67

# What a Rainbow World!

Look out the window and spot something green. Now find something blue. Where is something black? Can you find something yellow, purple, and orange, too?

If we look outside, we can usually see a whole bunch of colors. Which color is your favorite?

What a colorful world God has made! Think of all the colors on you right now. Ask someone to tell you all the colors they see in your eyes. Look into someone's eyes. How many colors can you find?

Sometimes November seems like a dull month. But see what beautiful colors you've found!

# Dear Jesus,

Thank You for all the colors, especially my favorite color, ＿＿＿ . Amen.

*God first loved us.* 1 John 4:19

# No Friends

"Mommy, Mommy," Jaimie came into the house, crying.

"Mommy, Mommy," Jaimie repeated, "Kate says my hair looks wilted. She won't let me swing in her yard."

Jaimie's mom looked up and smiled. "It does look like you need a shampoo tonight. Is that all that's wrong?"

"Is that all?" Jaimie wailed. "It's terrible . . . horrible . . . awful! I won't ever go to her house again. Now who can I play with?"

How do you feel when someone is mean to you? Have you ever been mean to anyone?

Jesus loves you even when others aren't nice. He forgives you even when you aren't nice. Jesus is the best Friend for us all.

# Dear Jesus,

Prayer suggestion: Thank Jesus now for your friends.

*Let us kneel before the Lord,*
*our Maker.* Psalm 95:6

# A Brown Day

"I don't like the color outside," said Stephanie as she looked out the window. "Everything looks brown in fall."

Grandpa came over to look, too. The empty tree branches were brown. The grass had turned brown. Even the leaves that blew on the ground had lost their bright fall colors. Stephanie was right; it was a brown world.

"Look, Grandpa, there goes a squirrel across the telephone wire," said Stephanie. "He's carrying something in his mouth." (What do you think the squirrel had?)

"It looks like it's something to bury until winter comes," said Grandpa. "I'll bet that squirrel will be glad to see that brown, round thing a few months from now. See how the squirrel is digging up those brown leaves? The leaves will be a good blanket for that bit of food. And see the squirrel's nice, thick, brown coat of fur?"

"You're right, Grandpa," Stephanie said. "Brown isn't a rainbow color, but I'm glad God made brown in our backyard."

# Dear Jesus,

Thank You for making our world so colorful. Amen.

*When this first census took place,*
*Quirinius was the governor of*
*Syria.* Luke 2:1–7

## *When?*

"Did Jesus live before the Pilgrims?" Asad asked his dad.

"Oh, yes, a long time before the Pilgrims," Dad answered.

"Did Jesus live before the cowboys?" Asad asked.

"Oh, yes, a long time before the cowboys," Dad answered.

"Well, when was Jesus born?" Asad asked.

"We don't know exactly when He was born," his dad answered, "but we know for sure that Jesus was born."

Christmas will be coming soon. That's when we celebrate Jesus' birthday. Listen to the story of Jesus' birth in the Bible.

## *Dear Jesus,*

Thank You for being born to be my Savior. Amen.

*Whoever welcomes this child*
*in My name, welcomes Me.*
Luke 9:46–48

# All Kinds of Shoes

Today we're going to play a word game. First, some questions; then, a riddle. Ready?

• The weather is cold and snowy where Martina lives. What will she wear on her feet today? _____

• It rained all night where Carlos lives. It's still raining. How will he dress to go outside? _____

• The temperature is very high and the sun is shining brightly at Edward's house. What will he wear on his feet? _____

• Now, here's the riddle: How are Martina, Carlos, and Edward alike? _____

Jesus loves them all. Jesus loves children who go barefoot like Edward, who wear boots like Carlos, and who wear warm winter boots like Martina. What do you have on your feet now? _____

Name some children Jesus loves: _____
_____ .

# Dear Jesus,

I know You love everybody. I know You love me. You love me when I wear tennis shoes, Sunday shoes, or what I have on my feet right now, _____ . Amen.

*Mary got ready.* Luke 1:39–45

## *A Birthday Is to Share*

It was almost Donzell's birthday. He was so excited! Donzell and his father were going to shop for party things. (What do you think they would buy?)

Donzell thought of all the fun he would have at the party. But he was also sad about his party. His best friend couldn't come.

Donzell knew the birthday would still be nice. But he was disappointed that his friend wouldn't share the fun.

"Birthdays are better if you share them," his dad said. "That's what is so great about Jesus' birthday. So many people can share Christmas."

Donzell's dad was right. And people are already sharing. We hear Christmas music. The Christmas decorations look so pretty.

Jesus' birthday is still a few weeks away, but how are you getting ready?

## *Dear Jesus,*

Your birthday is coming and I'm so _____ . Please help me remember the most important thing about Christmas: that You were born on the first Christmas. Amen.

*I am going to prepare a place
for you.* John 14:1–4

# Happy in Heaven

When you get into the car, where do you like to go? Do you like to ride to a special place to eat? Is there someone you like to visit?

Someday we will go to the most wonderful place. Someday we will go to heaven.

We don't know exactly what heaven will be like, but it will have everything we need to be happy.

Scott hopes he won't have any allergies in heaven. Dixie wants to eat lots of food in heaven and not get fat. Mia just wants to be happy.

And we will be happy in heaven. That's what Jesus promises us.

What makes you happy? How will your face look when you see Jesus in heaven?

# Dear Jesus,

I will be happy to come to heaven. When I see You in heaven, I will want to tell You all about _____
_____ . Amen.

*The Protector . . . never*
*dozes or sleeps.* Psalm 121:2–4

# Good Night

It was time to stop playing. Time to put on pajamas. Time to brush teeth. Time to read a book. Time to lie down. What time was it?

Is bedtime a good time for you? Sometimes it feels nice to settle down after a busy day. Sometimes children don't like to clean up toys and stop the fun. You can feel different ways about going to bed on different days.

God made nighttime so we could all sleep. Our bodies get tired, and we need to rest. What are some sounds you hear at bedtime? Do you feel someone kiss you good night or the smoothness of the bed sheet?

Even though we go to sleep, Jesus is still awake. He even sends angels to watch over us. Jesus wants us to have a good night so we can have a good tomorrow. Sleep well tonight. Good night.

# Dear Jesus,

Thank You for nighttime and the chance to rest, and for keeping me safe when I sleep. Amen.

*God was making all mankind*
*His friends through Christ.*
2 Corinthians 5:19

# Real or Pretend?

Let's pretend to build a tower. Pretend to take one block at a time and put it on top. Count with me as you pretend to build the tower.

"One, two, three, four, five, six . . . whoops! Be careful. Seven, eight . . . it's getting taller . . . nine, ten . . . can you keep going?

What's going to happen to the tower soon? I heard a crash. What happened?

That's okay, the pretend tower fell. You can build another one later. You can imagine that you have blocks. Do you pretend to play other things, too?

One thing is real, and we don't have to pretend about it: Jesus loves us. Even though we can't see Jesus, He really cares about us. Jesus isn't pretend. He's real. We can imagine what He might look like. We can imagine how Jesus is dressed. But Jesus is real. He really loves us. Jesus is our Friend.

# Dear Jesus

Thank You for being You. Amen.

*A child lies quietly in its
mother's arms.* Psalm 131:2–3

# A True Story

This really happened.

One day Mommy was on the telephone. Jill and Mandy were goofing off. Jill jumped on the sofa and hit a table. She cried and cried. Her arm was broken, and it hurt a lot.

Jill's mommy took her to the hospital. Jill's daddy met them there. He held Jill. Jill kept crying.

Some people at the hospital took X-ray pictures of Jill's arm. A doctor put her arm in a cast. Then Jill went home. Jill's arm still hurt a lot. She started to feel better the next day.

On Sunday Jill's mommy and daddy went to church. They prayed to God and thanked Him for helping Jill. What do you think Jill prayed about?

# Dear Jesus,

Sometimes I get hurt. Sometimes accidents happen. Sometimes I just goof off. Please give me people to help take care of me. I know I can always talk to You about how I feel. Amen.

*There was a wedding.*
John 2:1–2

# *Happy Times*

What an exciting day! There was going to be a wedding at church.

People started arriving. Some were all dressed up. Everyone sat quietly. Then the organ started playing. A white cloth was pulled down the aisle. The wedding started.

Everything was lovely. There were lots of flowers. Everybody looked so happy! It was very exciting.

Now it was time for the reception. What a party! People danced and laughed and talked. Then it was time to go home.

Do you know someone who was in a wedding? Have you ever seen pictures of a wedding?

# *Dear Jesus,*

Thank You for some exciting times. Even though I'm not very old, there are some things I will remember a long, long time. Thank You for the wonderful time I had when _____
_____ . Amen.

*God showed His love
for us.* 1 John 4:9

# A Frosty Picture

Mario could hardly see through the window. Frost covered the glass. He started to draw a picture with his finger. Christmas was coming soon, so he drew a Christmas scene.

Take your finger and draw a Christmas picture in the air. Let's start with the stable. Now we need some people. Are you going to add animals? Keep working until your picture is done.

Mario's finger is getting wet and cold. Now he's done. Are you almost finished?

Oh, no! Mario's picture is starting to drip with water. There goes a cow. Now he can't see the manger at all. But he will still remember what is important about Christmas. Even without his frosty picture, Mario knows that Jesus was born at Christmas.

# Dear Jesus,

Prayer suggestion: What is the most important thing for you about Christmas? Thank Jesus for that.

*Tell others that the Father*
*sent His Son.* 1 John 4:14

# Happy Birthday, Dear Jesus

Christmas was coming! Today Brian was helping his mom get ready for a "Jesus birthday party." She was fixing the cake today.

First, Brian's mom made the batter. After the cake was baked and had cooled, Brian picked out his favorite frosting. (What kind of frosting would you choose?)

Then Brian put on the candles. (How many candles would you put on a "Jesus birthday cake"?)

Brian put 13 on the cake. That's because he found 13 candles in the box.

Soon his friends would come to celebrate Jesus' birthday. Brian had invited some children who didn't know much about Jesus. He wanted to tell them all about Christmas.

Whom could you invite to a "Jesus birthday party"?

# Dear Jesus,

I know all about Christmas. I know You were born in a manger. I know that shepherds and Wise Men visited You. Not everybody knows about Your birthday. Help me think of people I could tell about You. And happy birthday, dear Jesus! Amen.

*God has been gracious
to you.* Luke 1:30–33

# How Do You Open Up Christmas?

Duncan woke up slowly. The December air was cool, even underneath the bedcovers. Suddenly Duncan was ready to jump out of bed. He had remembered something. Today was the day to open Christmas!

"When can we open Christmas, Mommy?" he asked right away.

"Later, Duncan, later," his mom replied.

Later in the morning Duncan asked again, "Is it time now to open Christmas?"

"Not yet," his mom answered.

"Is it time to open Christmas *now?*" Duncan asked again and again. Always the answer was the same: not yet.

Finally, it was time.

Mommy stood on a ladder to reach the box from the top of the hall closet. Finally, the box was on the floor.

"Now, Duncan. Now you may open Christmas," his mom said.

Quickly but carefully Duncan unwound the thick strings that tied the box. He pulled off layers of newspaper. Then slowly, ever so slowly, he took out the pieces. A shepherd was on top. Then an empty manger. Next an angel. Finally the box was empty.

As Duncan arranged the figures on the table, he smiled. "Now that we've opened Christmas, it will feel like Christmas."

How do you open Christmas at your house?

# Dear Jesus,

Help me remember that Christmas is Your birthday. Amen.

*God sent His own Son.*
Galatians 4:4–5

# An Empty Christmas?

Jackie carried the tray carefully. The cookies looked so pretty! She and her dad had worked hard in the kitchen. They mixed the dough, then rolled it out. Jackie used Christmas cutters to make the fancy shapes. Now the cookies were baked, frosted, and decorated. She carried the tray slowly up her neighbor's steps.

"Why, Jackie! How nice to see you," said Mrs. Fritz. Mrs. Fritz lived alone near Jackie's house. Sometimes Jackie would visit her or talk with her as she swept the stairs. "How special to have cookies for Christmas," she smiled.

Jackie looked around the apartment. Things were just the same as always. There wasn't a Christmas tree. There were no decorations. No presents were stacked up. A small manger scene was the only thing different.

"Oh, Mrs. Fritz," said Jackie. "Your Christmas is empty. Where are your presents? Don't you have any decorations?"

"No, Jackie," said Mrs. Fritz. "This year there aren't any of those things for me. But see the manger?" Mrs. Fritz asked. "That's all I need for a good Christmas."

How do you feel hearing about Mrs. Fritz? Was she right about Christmas?

# Dear Jesus,

Thank You for all the wonderful things that make Christmas fun. Thanks especially for being born. Amen.

*She will have a son, and you*
*will name Him Jesus.*
Matthew 1:20—23

# The Smell of Christmas

Can you smell Christmas coming? What is the smell of Christmas at your house? Take a good sniff.

What were the smells of the first Christmas? Pretend you are in the stable with Mary and Joseph. Can you smell the animals? the hay? the warmth?

The smells of our Christmas celebration are different from the smells of the first Christmas Day. But there's something that is still the same: Christmas is still Jesus' birthday.

Christmas will always be Jesus' birthday.

# Dear Jesus,

We're getting ready to celebrate Your birthday at our house. We can almost smell Christmas coming. I'm so glad You were born at Christmas. Amen.

*So let us not become tired of
doing good.* Galatians 6:9–10

# Sharing Can Be Tough

Sharon was sorting through her toys. She wasn't happy about it, though.

The church was collecting toys for children who wouldn't have a Christmas present. Everyone was to bring something they didn't use anymore.

Sharon liked everything. She couldn't give away the big dump truck because she used that in the sand.

The big stack of puzzles would be fun to use on a gloomy day in winter.

Her dolls needed to sleep with her, even if they couldn't all fit on the bed.

"Sharon, what did you find?" her dad called. "I'll help you wrap it up."

What did Sharon say?

# Dear Jesus,

Sometimes sharing is so hard. Sometimes I want to keep everything for myself and don't even want to let somebody play with my toys. Then I don't even like to share _____ . Please help me to share better. Amen.

*Martha was upset.* Luke 10:38–42

# *When Shoes Don't Fit*

Amanda was very excited. She was going to the Christmas service at church. She wore her favorite outfit. Her hair looked so nice. Now she would put on her shiny shoes.

"Oh, Mommy," Amanda cried. "My shoes are too tight."

Amanda tried to squeeze her feet into the shoes. Then her mom helped, too. It didn't work. The shoes really were too tight.

"You'll just have to wear your other pair, Amanda," said her mom. "It's almost time to go."

"I can't wear those shoes," cried Amanda. "Everybody will laugh at my feet."

What do you think happened?

# *Dear Jesus,*

Everything doesn't always work out right. Everything doesn't always fit together. I get so upset sometimes! Please help me remember what's really important: that You love me. Amen.

*The Spirit produces love, joy,*
*peace, patience . . .* Galatians 5:22

# A Don't Day or a Do Day?

It was two o'clock.

"Ouch," said Sammy.

"Sammy, *don't* touch that holly decoration; it's sharp."

It was three o'clock.

"Mommy," Sammy said, "the lights just went out on the Christmas tree."

"Sammy, *don't* play with the cord. *Don't* go near those electric wires."

It was four o'clock.

Crash went the tin of Christmas cookies. (Guess what room Sammy was in now.)

"Sammy, *don't* get into those Christmas goodies. *Don't* go near the kitchen," said Daddy.

Don't, don't, don't. For Sammy it seemed like a *don't* day instead of a Christmastime day.

Sammy could have remembered the do's about Christmas. Let's help Sammy.

"*Do* show kindness, like the shepherds showed baby Jesus. Sammy, *do* make a Christmas picture to give to someone.

"*Do* show love, like Mary and Joseph showed to baby Jesus. Sammy, *do* nice things, like picking up the toys and offering to help."

What else could Sammy *do?*

# Dear Jesus,

Help me *do* loving things for others. Amen.

*You know the way that leads to
the place where I am. . . .*
John 14:1–4

# Window Shopping

"I want this," said Marie as she walked through the aisles of toys.
"Buy me this," begged Marie as she passed the building blocks.
"Look at that neat airplane," said Marie. "Can't I have that?"

Sometimes walking through a toy store before Christmas isn't much fun. You can't get everything you want.

Jesus gives us something for Christmas that we can't find in a store. It's not hiding behind the dolls. It's not between the covers of the new books.

His present is that someday we will live with Him in heaven.

Even if we had money to buy all the toys in a store, we couldn't buy Jesus' gift. That's because His gift is a present. There isn't any checkout counter. There isn't any wrapping. And Jesus' present doesn't cost a single penny. He gives us heaven, free.

# Dear Jesus,

I love to look at all the toys in the stores. Things look so pretty, all ready for Christmas. Help me remember that Your present is coming some other time. Please help me be patient. Amen.

*You did not choose Me;*
*I chose you.* John 15:16–17

# Puddles

It had rained and rained and rained. The ground was soaking wet. You could almost hear the earth go "slurp, slurp." Because there was a lot of rain, there were also a lot of puddles.

What do you think about puddles? Do you ever do anything with puddles?

Tara was going outside. She wore her boots and took an umbrella. It had stopped raining, but she took her new umbrella anyway.

When Tara got outside, she headed for the biggest puddle. Splash, splash, splash. Tromp, tromp, tromp. Smush, smush, smush. What do you think Tara was doing?

Pretty soon Tara was so wet she went back to the house.

What do you think happened next?

# Dear Jesus,

Sometimes it's hard to make decisions. I know what I should do, but sometimes I don't. Help me think about my choices, and help me do what is right. Amen.

*God . . . made His light shine
in our hearts.* 2 Corinthians 4:6

# Nothing to Do

Glenn walked around the house. He looked in the bedroom. He walked to the kitchen. Then Glenn walked upstairs.

"Daddy, there's nothing to do," he complained.

"Why, Glenn! What about the things you got for Christmas?" his dad asked.

"I'm tired of those," Glenn answered. "And I need new batteries."

"Why don't you rearrange the manger?" Dad suggested.

"No; Christmas is over and I don't feel like it anyway," Glenn answered.

"Change the Christmas tree ornaments. You can move them around and make the tree look different," Dad said.

"No, no, no! Christmas is over. I don't even feel like Christmas anymore," Glenn said.

Do you feel like Glenn today? What could you suggest for Glenn to do?

# Dear Jesus,

I know Christmas Day is finished. Help me remember to keep thanking You for coming at Christmas. Amen.

*Jesus grew.* Luke 2:52

# Growing Up and Up

I used to be one,
And I had such fun.
(Do something you could do as a one-year-old).

I used to be two;
See what I could do.
(Do something you could do as a two-year-old).

I used to be three;
Take a look at growing-up me!
(Do something like a three-year-old).

You've grown a lot since you were a baby. Who are some of the people who helped you grow? Those people used to be little, too. Everybody starts out as a baby.

Even Jesus was a baby; then a one-year-old; then a two-year-old; and He was even as old as you are now!

# Dear Jesus,

I'm glad You know how it feels to grow up. Amen.

*Jesus Christ is the same . . .*
Hebrews 13:8

# Good-bye

"Good-bye," Johanna said sadly to her grandma. "I wish you didn't have to go."

"Good-bye," Hank waved through the car window. Hank waved to his old house. He was moving away.

"Good-bye," Justin waved to his teacher. "See you next week."

Have you waved good-bye to someone today? Let's see how you wave good-bye.

We are all waving good-bye to something today: an old year. Tomorrow we start a new calendar. We can wave hello to a new year tomorrow.

Waving good-bye can be happy. Waving good-bye can be sad—or a little happy and a little sad.

If you waved to Jesus, it wouldn't be for hello or good-bye. Because Jesus is always with us.

# Dear Jesus,

I don't have to say good-bye to You this year because You're always with me. I like that. Amen.

# Scripture Index

page

**GENESIS**
1:9–10 .................... 152
1:31 ....................... 89
2:2–3 ..................... 156
2:8–9 ..................... 100
2:19 ....................... 79
7:1–16 ..................... 97
8:1–5 ...................... 98
8:22 ...................... 129
9:12–17 ............... 94, 181
37:4 ...................... 120

**EXODUS**
16:4a ..................... 165
20:12 ..................... 217

**JOB**
37:1–5 ..................... 29
38:39–39:1 ................ 114

**PSALMS**
8:1, 3–4 ................... 22
9:1–2 ...................... 61
17:8 ...................... 211
24:1 ...................... 108
26:8 ...................... 192
34:7 ....................... 96
40:11 ..................... 207
44:8 ...................... 124
50:11 ...................... 39
50:15 ..................... 224
51:1–2 .................... 173
67 ....................... 229
68:9 ....................... 64
74:16–17 ............. 107, 138
77:11–12 ................... 19
78:1–4 .................... 166
86:3–5 .................... 197
90:1–2 ............... 180, 193
91:11–12 ................... 80
92:1 .................. 26, 149
92:12–14 .................. 112
95:6 ...................... 231
103:11–13 ................. 219
104:10–28 ................. 103
104:14–15 ................. 123
104:24 .................... 148
106:1–2 ................... 143
108:4 ..................... 147
111:4 ...................... 53

116:1–2 .................... 59
118:24 ..................... 48
118:29 ..................... 13
119:105 ........... 37, 144, 206
121 ....................... 50
121:1–2 ................... 179
121:2–4 ................... 236
121:7–8 ................... 134
122:1 ......... 16, 132, 175, 200
130:1–2, 5 ................. 33
130:5–6 ................... 215
131:2–3 ............... 92, 238
136:1 ................. 182, 227
136:1–3 ................... 111
145:1–3 ................... 145
145:8–9 .................... 86
145:13b–16 ................ 154
145:15–16 .................. 31
146:5–6 ................... 125
147:16–17 ................. 162
149:1–3 .................... 27

**PROVERBS**
13:13 ...................... 35
16:15 .................. 60, 99
16:20 ..................... 106
17:17 ..................... 121
18:15 ...................... 58
18:24 ...................... 24
20:12 ...................... 93
24:5 ...................... 137

**ECCLESIASTES**
12:1a ..................... 110

**ISAIAH**
12:2–6 .................... 168
35:1–2 ..................... 67
42:16 ..................... 190
49:15 ...................... 14
55:10–11 ................... 63
64:8 ....................... 65

**JEREMIAH**
5:24b ..................... 189
17:7–8 .................... 185

**JONAH**
4:5–7 ..................... 188

## MATTHEW

| | |
|---|---|
| 1:20–23 | 244 |
| 2:1–2 | 17 |
| 2:1–2, 9–11 | 178 |
| 2:9–11 | 18 |
| 6:26–27 | 85 |
| 7:7–8 | 172 |
| 8:23–27 | 23 |
| 10:2–10 | 170 |
| 10:29–31 | 196 |
| 11:28 | 155 |
| 13:55 | 139 |
| 14:22–23 | 218 |
| 18:1–4 | 223 |
| 28:1–7 | 74 |
| 28:19–20 | 221 |
| 28:20b | 133 |

## MARK

| | |
|---|---|
| 4:3–8 | 82 |
| 4:35–39 | 122 |
| 6:45–51 | 69 |
| 10:13–16 | 222 |
| 16:1–8 | 75 |

## LUKE

| | |
|---|---|
| 1:30–33 | 242 |
| 1:39–45 | 234 |
| 1:46–55 | 183 |
| 2:1–7 | 232 |
| 2:7 | 95 |
| 2:19 | 66 |
| 2:25–35 | 195 |
| 2:41 | 136 |
| 2:52 | 251 |
| 9:46–48 | 233 |
| 10:30–35 | 70 |
| 10:38–42 | 246 |
| 11:9–10 | 51 |
| 21:1–4 | 40 |
| 24:1–9 | 72, 78 |
| 24:28–34 | 73 |

## JOHN

| | |
|---|---|
| 1:40–42 | 213 |
| 1:43–46 | 20 |
| 1:45–46 | 220 |
| 2:1–2 | 239 |
| 3:5–8 | 187 |
| 3:16 | 34, 109 |
| 3:17 | 68, 126 |
| 6:5–13 | 203 |
| 10:14–16 | 57 |
| 11:25–26 | 146 |

| | |
|---|---|
| 11:25–27 | 71 |
| 11:32–36 | 199 |
| 14:1–4 | 235, 248 |
| 14:2 | 113 |
| 14:4–6 | 127 |
| 15:4–7 | 210 |
| 15:9 | 54, 83, 151 |
| 15:12–13 | 176 |
| 15:16–17 | 249 |
| 19:17–18 | 21 |
| 20:1–10 | 77 |
| 20:11–18 | 76 |
| 20:30–31 | 205 |

## ACTS

| | |
|---|---|
| 1:8 | 128, 198 |
| 9:36–42 | 49 |
| 10:37–43 | 177 |
| 16:22–34 | 171 |
| 22:16 | 214 |

## ROMANS

| | |
|---|---|
| 5:6–8 | 52 |
| 5:8 | 202 |
| 8:38–39 | 38 |
| 10:8 | 141 |

## 1 CORINTHIANS

| | |
|---|---|
| 1:1–3 | 163 |
| 1:18 | 55 |
| 15:3–7 | 81 |
| 15:20 | 115 |
| 15:20–22 | 157 |
| 16:2 | 208 |

## 2 CORINTHIANS

| | |
|---|---|
| 1:19–20 | 158 |
| 4:6 | 250 |
| 5:17 | 204 |
| 5:19 | 237 |
| 9:7–8 | 150 |
| 13:11–14 | 186 |

## GALATIANS

| | |
|---|---|
| 2:20 | 104 |
| 4:4–5 | 32, 243 |
| 4:4–7 | 131 |
| 5:22 | 247 |
| 6:2 | 130 |
| 6:9–10 | 245 |

## EPHESIANS

| | |
|---|---|
| 2:19 | 84 |
| 4:10 | 62 |

4:32 .......................... 56
5:20 .......................... 119
6:1–4 ........................ 41
6:18 .......................... 105

PHILIPPIANS
4:4 ........................... 209

COLOSSIANS
1:1–4 ........................ 46
1:20 .......................... 102
3:12–13 ...................... 91
3:15–17 ...................... 164
3:20 .......................... 15

1 THESSALONIANS
5:16–18 ................. 118, 140

2 THESSALONIANS
3:8–9 ........................ 142
3:16 .......................... 167

1 TIMOTHY
4:4–5 ........................ 174

2 TIMOTHY
3:15 .......................... 153
3:15–17 ...................... 42

HEBREWS
13:8 .......................... 252

JAMES
2:18 .......................... 28

1 PETER
5:6–7 ........................ 117

1 JOHN
1:3 ........................... 201
2:12 .......................... 184
3:1a ................... 30, 160
4:7 ................. 43, 87, 194
4:9 ........................... 240
4:9–10 ................. 44, 88
4:10 .......................... 225
4:10–11 ...................... 135
4:11 ................... 45, 228
4:12 ................... 36, 90
4:14 .......................... 241
4:18 .......................... 226
4:19 .......................... 230
4:19–21 ...................... 169
5:11–13 ...................... 161

REVELATION
1:4–6 ........................ 191
2:10c ......................... 47
3:20–21 ...................... 212
7:16–17 ...................... 25
14:13 ......................... 101
21:1–4 ........................ 159
21:3–4 ........................ 216
21:10–21 ...................... 116

*255*

# Devotions for Special Days

Baby, New in Home    195, (223)
Birthday    30, 111
Broken Arm    238;    Leg    145
Christmas    243, 246, 250
    Getting Ready for    232, 234, 240–242, 244, 247
Death    34, 146, 199
    Worry About    71, 157
Easter    75–78, 81
    Preparing for    59, 72–74
Epiphany    17, 18
Eyeglasses    93
Fear
    of Dark    80, 102, 187
    of Halloween Costumes    211
    of House Fire    50
    of Nightmares    23
    of Parental Sickness    117
    of Parental Worries    224
    of Stormy Weather    29, 37, 69, 140
Halloween    205, 207, 211, 212
Heaven    25, 34, 159, 191, 235
Moving/New Home    133
New Year    13, 252
Pet, Loss of    114
Piano Practice    91
Rainbow    94
School, Getting Ready for    174, 179
Sharing    58, 226, 245
Sickness    70, 192
Thanksgiving Day    225–227
Thumb Sucking    92
Tooth Loose    26
Vacation Trip    42, 127, 141, 146, 186
Valentine's Day    43, 45–47, 53
Wedding    239